SOLVING THE
HOMEWORK PROBLEM BY
FLIPPING
THE LEARNING

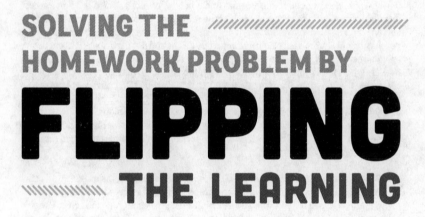

SOLVING THE HOMEWORK PROBLEM BY FLIPPING THE LEARNING

ASCD

Alexandria, Virginia USA

1703 N. Beauregard St. • Alexandria, VA 22311-1714 USA
Phone: 800-933-2723 or 703-578-9600 • Fax: 703-575-5400
Website: www.ascd.org • E-mail: member@ascd.org
Author guidelines: www.ascd.org/write

Deborah S. Delisle, *Executive Director;* Stefani Roth, *Publisher;* Genny Ostertag, *Director, Content Acquisitions;* Julie Houtz, *Director, Book Editing & Production;* Joy Scott Ressler, *Editor;* Masie Chong, *Graphic Designer;* Mike Kalyan, *Director, Production Services;* Cynthia Stock, *Typesetter;* Kelly Marshall, *Production Specialist*

PAPERBACK ISBN: 978-1-4166-2372-4   ASCD product #117012   n4/17
PDF E-BOOK ISBN: 978-1-4166-2374-8; see Books in Print for other formats.

Quantity discounts are available: e-mail programteam@ascd.org or call 800-933-2723, ext. 5773, or 703-575-5773. For desk copies, go to www.ascd.org/deskcopy.

Library of Congress Cataloging-in-Publication Data

22 21 20 19 18 17   1 2 3 4 5 6 7 8 9 10 11 12

SOLVING THE //////////////////////////////
HOMEWORK PROBLEM BY
FLIPPING
////////////// THE LEARNING

DEDICATION

I am not a self-made man and only hope that I can live my life in a way that honors those I have built into my life. I acknowledge two of them here.

To Eddie Anderson, my high school chemistry teacher, who inspired me to become a teacher. You saw something in a geeky teenager that inspired me to teach high school chemistry for 24 years and to somehow live up to your legacy.

To Virgil Gosser, my mentor, friend, and supervising teacher during my years as a student teacher. You showed me the power of positive relationships with students. Your faith in me and in God is a continual source of inspiration to me.

01

CHAPTER 1

THE CASE FOR FLIPPED HOMEWORK

Homework! The word strikes fear and trepidation in students. It truly is the "H" word. Parents have a love-hate relationship with homework. They want what is best for their kids, and many think it is the way for their children to succeed, but they fear that they may not be able to help their children. Teachers feel an obligation to assign homework because of outside pressure, internal motivation, or simply because we have always done it this way. What is the value of homework? Does it help students, hinder students, or is it an instrument of control teachers hold over students? As a teacher, I have assigned a lot of homework. Some homework assignments have been meaningful and effective, while other assignments have merely been busywork that did not help my students. And as a parent of three children, I have spent countless hours working with my kids. I have sometimes seen how homework benefits my children and other times seen how it hinders their education. With each of my three children, there have been moments of tears when I questioned the value and purpose of a homework assignment.

According to the National Center for Family Literacy, in 2013 (Scoon, 2013) 50 percent of parents say they have trouble helping their kids with homework. The reasons they gave were:

- They don't understand the material (46.5 percent).
- Their kids don't want help (31.6 percent).
- They are too busy (21.9 percent).

I received this e-mail from Barbra Sterns (2016, personal correspondence), a corporate trainer and frustrated parent:

As far as I am concerned, the "H" word is the biggest advantage of the flipped classroom. When my kids were in school, six or seven different teachers would each lecture for an hour and then send the kids home to do the homework, which was almost always application and practice of the concepts from class that day.

But my kids didn't come straight home; they went to day care until I was back from work. I dropped them off at day care at 7:30 a.m. and picked them up at 5:30–6:00 p.m. The day care didn't have willing or trained helpers for homework. Even after-school programs at the school used their time for activity and fun, not to extend the school day. Then in the three hours between the time we got home and the time they went to bed, we fit in meals, baths, martial arts, birthdays, etc. Homework was always a battle; they couldn't always remember well enough to apply and when I tried to help they said, "That's not what my teacher told me."

THE PROBLEM WITH HOMEWORK

From my lens as both a career teacher and a father, I see several problems with homework in today's educational climate:

- Homework that seemingly has little meaning and usefulness
- Assignments that take too long to complete
- Assignments that many students don't complete
- Teachers sending students home with assignments that they are ill-prepared to complete
- Ineffective homework assignments

Denise Pope, PhD, a researcher at Stanford University, surveyed more than 4,300 students at high-achieving secondary schools and found that only 20 to 30 percent of students found their homework to be useful and meaningful (Pope, 2013). Homework, in many cases, does not help students achieve, does not help students develop curiosity, and may be an exercise in compliance and control. Assignments are often given without context, are either too easy or too difficult, or are irrelevant to the course.

As a parent, I have watched my children work late into the night, and even into the wee hours of the morning, to complete homework. It feels as if some teachers equate the amount of homework with rigor. But in reality, all their homework accomplishes is teaching students to resent and sabotage the love of learning.

The Educator's Dilemma

For a variety of reasons, students often come to class without having completed the necessary prework. Should teachers fight this, or should they give up and not assign any homework? If our goal is compliance instead of learning, then we educators have missed the point of homework. On the flip side, hard work and perseverance are elements of learning. Not every student is interested in everything that is taught, and many may lack the internal motivation to complete all assignments.

A Recipe for Failure

I am the first to confess that I sent students home with assignments that some *could not* complete. I sent them home with work they were incapable of completing with the limited background I had given them. Maybe they did not have the cognitive framework, maybe they did not have adequate support at home, or maybe they were simply too busy with the demands of their home life. Some students came to class with incomplete work because they saw no value to the assignment and chose not to complete it. Others had been inundated with senseless homework over many years and rejected homework as a whole on principle. Much of the time, students didn't complete homework assignments because they lacked the necessary background knowledge and gave up. Then these same students came to class and professed not to care about school and often became discipline problems. In my experience, students who are discipline problems are getting negative attention for behavior to mask feelings of inadequacy and a sense of failure. It is easier to struggle and disregard the value of school than to struggle, continue to care, and feel like a failure.

The Great Debate

There is quite a debate among educators, parents, and communities about the value of homework. On one side are the proponents of homework, who feel that students need to have time to practice what they have learned in class. And on the other side are those who think homework is a waste of time or harmful for children. Some parents believe that schools should not assign *any* homework. To those parents, school is for learning and home is for family. They feel that school is infringing on the homelife of families and want academic work to be restricted to the school day. I sympathize with these parents because, as a parent myself, I too have seen the dark side of homework, wherein my children are lost, frustrated, or have been given so much homework that sleep is sacrificed.

For some teachers, homework is assigned because it is expected. Little deep thought is given to the quantity, quality, or efficacy of the assignment. And for others, homework can be a power issue, whereby teachers use homework as a reward-and-punishment system to control students. A quick review of the research can be summarized by the work of two educators—Robert Marzano and Alfie Kohn.

Marzano. Robert Marzano evaluated the research on homework and came to the conclusion that homework is an effective tool for learning. Marzano found a correlation between the age of the student and the effectiveness of homework. The older the student, the greater the effect on student achievement. His findings are summarized in Figure 1.1.

FIGURE 1.1
STUDENT AGE AND EFFECTIVENESS OF HOMEWORK

GRADE LEVEL	PERCENTILE GAIN
4–6	+6
7–9	+12
10–12	+24

Marzano also suggested an ideal amount of time for students to engage in homework, which he refers to as the "ten-minute rule." Per the rule, students should be assigned no more than ten minutes of homework per grade level. So, following that rule, a 4th grade student should have no more than forty minutes of homework every night.

Kohn. The other side of the homework debate can be represented by Alfie Kohn. Like Marzano, Kohn examined the research. However, unlike Marzano, Kohn concluded that the research shows that homework has little effect on student achievement and should be abolished. He stated in an online video (Kohn, 2009):

When you think about it, it's kinda weird that after spending all day in school, kids are asked to do more academic assignments when they get home. What is weirder about this is that we don't think it is weird. We never stop to ask if it is logical, whether it is consistent with our ultimate goals for children's development, or whether any research supports it. The questions I want to ask about homework are not the little bitty questions like should we cap it at x minutes? I want to ask the question, "Why do kids need to work a second shift when they get home on academic assignments?"

Kohn argues that students need more unstructured time to play, explore, and develop outside of the structure of rigorous homework. Kohn criticizes homework studies and questions the value of any homework. In his book, *The Homework Myth*, he concludes that ". . . the research offers no reason to believe that students in high-quality classrooms whose teachers give little or no homework would be at a disadvantage as regards any meaningful kind of learning." He breaks down his summary into two categories: younger students and older students. He states that for younger students, there is either no relationship, and possibly even a negative relationship, between homework and student achievement. For older students, Kohn states that there is no significant relationship between homework and student achievement, with one exception: there is a positive relationship between the amount of homework done and students' grades (Kohn 2006).

A Possible Solution?

So which is it? Does homework benefit students? As a classroom teacher, as someone who has visited classrooms around the globe, and as one who has reviewed the literature, I have come to the conclusion that homework, *when done with meaning and forethought*, helps students achieve. Homework must be relevant, meaningful, and taught at a level that is commensurate with a student's ability.

Is there another way? What if homework took less time, was more meaningful, more relevant, more focused, and students actually did it? I have seen how flipped learning "solves" the homework problem. No longer is homework the "H" word, but rather an activity that prepares students to learn deeply and become active and engaged participants in the classroom experience.

FLIPPED LEARNING AND BLOOM'S TAXONOMY

Before discussing flipped learning, let's look at homework in light of Bloom's Taxonomy. In a traditional classroom, the lower tiers of Bloom's Taxonomy are done in class and students are sent home to climb their way to the top of the taxonomy by completing practice problems, projects, and papers on their own time without an expert present to help. In a flipped classroom, the lower tiers of Bloom's Taxonomy are delivered to the individual learner outside of the class, so all students can engage in higher-order thinking during class with their peers and an expert present.

From the Bottom Up

As I look back at my classes before I pioneered the flipped class with Aaron Sams (Bergmann and Sams, 2012), I spent the bulk of class time teaching remembering and understanding and then sent my students home to apply, analyze, evaluate, and create (see Figure 1.2). As a parent, I have had my children come home and get frustrated with homework. But my kids had me, a professional educator, there to help them, so my educational practice was adequate for my children. But not all children grow up in educator-rich homes.

Many students come to us from disadvantaged homes where parents lack the time or expertise to help their children. I especially remember how sending students home to do the "hard stuff" didn't work when I taught in an inner-city middle school in Denver, Colorado. When I sent students home to apply and analyze, many came

FIGURE 1.2
BLOOM'S TAXONOMY, EASY/HARD (ANDERSON 2001)

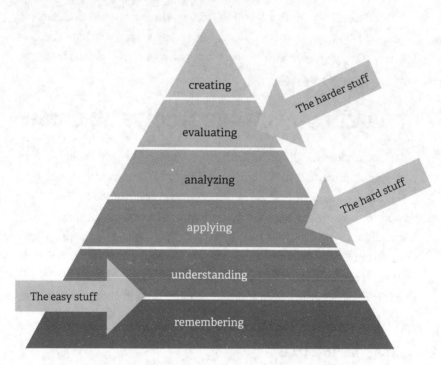

back empty-handed. Some of these students did not have the parental support at home to help them with the more difficult cognitive tasks and, thus, they were not successful. For instance, I recall teaching my 7th grade students the rock cycle via a lecture. Students were expected to take notes and then go home and answer some questions on a work-sheet. I was frustrated by both the lack-of-completion percentage and the quality of the students' answers. A typical assignment I might send home when I taught was:

"The mid-ocean ridge is a divergent boundary where lava erupts onto the ocean floor. Explain what is happening in terms of igneous rocks." This assignment requires students to understand the difference between extrusive igneous and intrusive igneous rocks. From a Bloom's Taxonomic lens, this is either at the application or analysis level. It is important to analyze, but expecting them to complete this assignment on their own with little or no help is unrealistic at best and harmful at worst.

From the Top Down: The Flipped Classroom

What if we were able to do the "hard stuff" in class and use the homework time for kids to get the basic knowledge and understanding? This is exactly what happens in a flipped classroom. The "hard stuff" is done in the presence of the most valuable resource in any classroom—the expert: the teacher! (See Figure 1.3.)

Let's flip Bloom's Taxonomy. Let's spend more class time on the more difficult cognitive tasks and less class time on the easier tasks. In

FIGURE 1.3
BLOOM'S TAXONOMY INVERTED

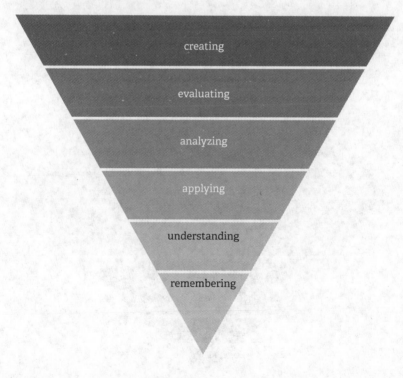

creating

evaluating

analyzing

applying

understanding

remembering

the diagram in Figure 1.2, consider each tier of the pyramid to be time spent on different tasks in class. Students need more time working on the higher tiers of Bloom's Taxonomy with their teacher present to help them with the lower tiers.

When I have shared the inverted Bloom's Taxonomy (Figure 1.3) with educators, they are overwhelmed with the amount of time spent in the top two tiers of the pyramid. They don't see how their students can spend that amount of time evaluating and creating. Instead, a more realistic picture of how flipped learning and Bloom's Taxonomy may intersect is a diamond (see Figure 1.4). Assuming again that the greater area represents

FIGURE 1.4
BLOOM'S TAXONOMY IN DIAMOND FORMAT

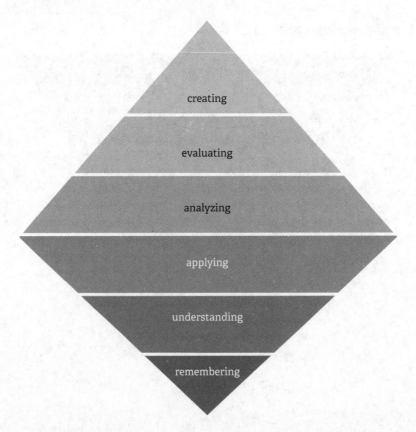

a greater amount of class time devoted to the level, the bulk of class time will be used for application and analysis.

For too long, schools have been upside down with regard to which tasks are done in class and which are done outside of class. Class time must be used more thoughtfully in ways that allow all students to receive the support they need both in and out of class. In doing so, all students benefit. In the Bloom's Taxonomy diamond model, flipping the class simplifies the learning process for students and teachers by placing the right resource—the teacher—with those with the greatest need—students struggling with higher-order tasks. Magdalen Radovich, an instructional leader in Middletown, New Jersey, says that the best thing about flipped learning is that "the light lifting happens at home and the heavy lifting happens in the class with the teacher present."

ENTER FLIPPED LEARNING

Flipped learning, at its core, is a very simple idea. Students interact with introductory material at home prior to coming to class. This usually takes the form of an instructional video created by the classroom teacher. This replaces the direct instruction, which is often referred to as a lecture, in the classroom. Classroom time is then repurposed for tasks such as projects, inquiry, debate, or simply working on class assignments that, in the old paradigm, would have been sent home. This simple time-shift is transforming classrooms around the globe.

A growing number of teachers have made homework more meaningful and effective by flipping their classrooms. At its core, the flipped classroom approach is very simple: direct instruction and basic content delivery is delivered to students through an instructional video (which I will call a flipped video) and then class time is devoted to application, analysis, and practice with the teacher present to clear up misconceptions and questions. Basically, the easy stuff is done before the face-to-face class time. Once the teacher and students are in the same room, the basic content has been introduced, and the repurposed class time is used to engage students in higher-order thinking. The students do the easy stuff before class and the hard stuff in class, where the teacher is there to help them.

HOW FLIPPED HOMEWORK BREAKS THE MOLD

How is flipped homework different than traditional homework? Interestingly, flipped homework flies in the face of some of the research on effective homework. Copper (2001) states that homework should never be used to teach new material. Instead, effective homework should be for practice and extension of the things learned during class. Flipped homework is, therefore, a paradigm shift in best homework practices. This radical departure from the traditional understanding is now possible because of the simple fact that a teacher's introductory lesson can be shared in an interactive and engaging way, whereby students can come to class with sufficient background knowledge. Thus, flipped homework not only turns homework on its head, but it also turns homework research on its head.

Flipped homework also solves the time problem. Some students may complete in 10 minutes an assignment that make take others an hour to complete. The beauty of a flipped video is that the time length is fixed. When the flipped class is done well, the videos are short and the length of the video is known. Though some students will take more time than others interacting with the flipped videos, the time differential is much less than with typical homework.

STUDENT PERCEPTIONS OF FLIPPED HOMEWORK

Students around the globe are learning in flipped classrooms. Flipped classrooms can be found in virtually every country, on every subject, and at every grade level. What are *students'* perceptions about the intersection of homework and flipped learning? In writing this book, I reached out to flipped classroom teachers around the globe and asked them to administer a survey to their students. I sent invitations to teachers I had worked with and even published requests through several social media outlets. This is not an action research survey where there are control groups and an established research protocol. However, the large number of student responses adds greatly to our understanding of student perception of flipped learning and specifically its relation to homework. If you want to see the original questionnaire, please go to bit.ly/fliphw. The data are interesting and compelling. I will share some of the results in this chapter and later in the book.

The survey was taken by 2,344 students (the majority of whom were from the United States; see Figure 1.5) and the breakdown of grade levels is shown in Figure 1.6. Students were in a variety of flipped courses (see Figure 1.7). The fact that there were 3,578 responses to the question posed in Figure 1.7 indicates that many students were in more than one flipped course.

FIGURE 1.5
COUNTRIES OF ORIGIN OF SURVEY RESPONDENTS

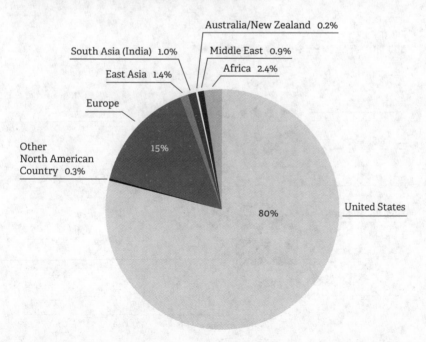

FIGURE 1.6
GRADE LEVELS OF SURVEY RESPONDENTS

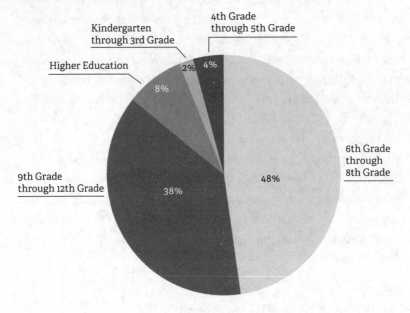

FIGURE 1.7
SUBJECTS TAKEN BY SURVEY RESPONDENTS

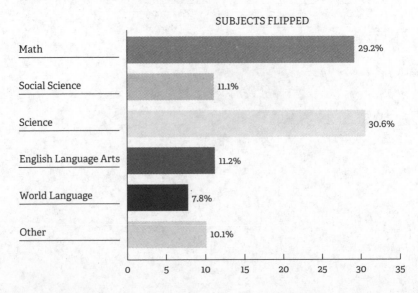

It is interesting that the majority of flipped classes were in science and mathematics. While this data might suggest that it is easier to flip science and math, I am not convinced of that. I believe classes in every subject can be flipped, with important modifications. That is one reason why Aaron Sams and I wrote the *Flipped Learning Series*, which includes separate books about how to flip in five different settings—Science, Math, English Language, Social Studies, and Elementary.

Students' responses to the question, "If you had a choice between a flipped class or a more traditional class, which would you choose?" are shown in Figure 1.8. Most prefer flipped learning or have no preference. Based on the added benefits cited elsewhere in this book, flipped learning is a model that should be considered deeply.

FIGURE 1.8
STUDENT RESPONSES REGARDING PREFERENCE FOR TRADITIONAL OR FLIPPED CLASSES

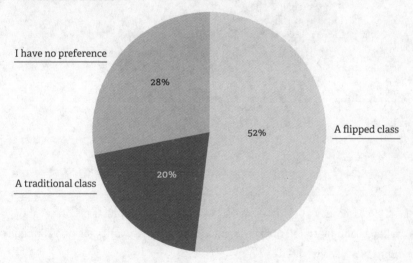

Screen Time and Flipped Videos

One criticism I sometimes hear is that flipped learning adds screen time for children who already spend too much time in front of a screen. I am sensitive to this issue, as I believe that children (and adults) spend far too much time in front of screens. And learning needs to take place in rich and engaging environments, not only in front of screens. I want students to walk away from their screens and go outside, play games, invent, ride bikes, and simply be kids. Thus, the question I asked was, "How does flipped video affect your total amount of screen time?" I was pleasantly surprised that, in many responses, students are replacing other screen time with a flipped homework assignment (see Figure 1.9).

FIGURE 1.9
STUDENT REPONSES REGARDING FLIPPED VIDEOS AND SCREEN TIME

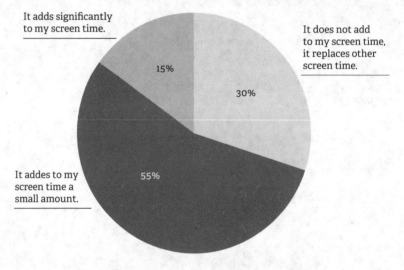

It adds significantly to my screen time.

It does not add to my screen time, it replaces other screen time.

15%

30%

It addes to my screen time a small amount.

55%

I closed out the survey with two open-ended questions, in which I asked students to tell me the disadvantages and advantages of a flipped homework assignment.

Disadvantages

A large percentage of students said that there were no disadvantages, with some being quite insistent about it. But there clearly are some challenges, as outlined in the following quotes from some of the 2,344 students surveyed:

- If you are confused, you have to wait till tomorrow or it takes a while and sometimes they don't help us, so sometimes it's really confusing.
- We can't ask questions while watching the video. We have to e-mail our teacher or wait until class the next day.
- Some of the disadvantages are that sometimes the video can be too long and I have less time for other subjects.
- I am a "hands-on learner" so I don't get it quite as much as I do at school.
- It is difficult to stay focused on the subject.
- I have to use my computer and my Wi-Fi is awful.
- If a student doesn't do a homework [assignment], they will not know what [is] going on, or if they are attempting to take notes and do not understand something, they cannot get another explanation that they might understand (unless the teacher lets you ask questions about the notes the next day, which our teacher does).
- Sometimes we need a teacher to teach us if we don't get it.

As I look at the responses above and the remainder of the survey, there were definitely students who had some difficulty accessing the content. This illustrates how important it is to ensure equitable access to a flipped video for all students. The other major theme is that students wanted help when they were first interacting with the content. Later in the book, I will share how these challenges are being addressed in greater detail.

Advantages

The students who found flipped homework assignments advantageous made the following remarks:

- We can do assignments at all hours of the day.
- You get to ask questions about homework while doing it in class.
- It helps us to do less work but understand better.

- When you watch the video first and then take notes and finally do the homework, then that makes it a whole lot easier and less stressful.
- I am more focused on the task and can learn at a better pace compared to when the teacher is teaching the entire classroom.
- You can re-watch the videos if you don't understand.
- It is easier to understand and the homework doesn't take as long.
- We have a chance to do homework inside and outside of school.
- You have time to think and it is easy for you to pass your assignments and assessments.
- My class has more time for discussion and my teacher can answer more questions that I have.
- Students do harder things in class, and I can have questions prepared for [my] teachers.
- You can do [the assignment] even if you are confused and then ask questions when you get to class, rather than not being able to do it at all.
- In a traditional classroom, the homework is a piece of paper that can easily be lost. But in a flipped class with electronic homework, we can retrieve the homework as long as we have access to a computer.
- It is a lot easier and you do [the assignment] on your own time and you learn at your own pace.

Students like having greater control of their learning. They like pausing and rewinding their teachers, they like having greater access to their teacher, and they like moving at their own pace. The survey shows an overwhelming preference for flipped homework assignments.

UNIVERSAL THEMES FROM STUDENTS

When I speak with students in flipped classrooms across the globe, it is notable that they rarely discuss the flipped videos. I have found that the following three themes often surface:

1. *Access to teachers.* Students need help from teachers and since there is more time for teachers to help kids, they get more help.

2. *Engaging class activities.* With more time in class, students report that the in-class activities connect to their learning. This adds purpose to the flipped video homework assignments. Students realize that if they do the homework, they are prepared to engage in meaningful activities in class.

3. *Collaborative time.* In a flipped class, students are usually working in small groups. Students find meaning through inter-acting and collaborating with their peers. Students like the time they have working in tandem with fellow learners.

Clearly, flipped learning is resonating with students, and they prefer it. During a recent episode of my radio show, I had the chance to inter-view Caroline Kurban, Director of the Center for Excellence in Learning and Teaching at MEF University in Istanbul, Turkey. The founder of MEF University, Dr. İbrahim Arıkan, was investigating innovative ways to deliver instruction when he came across flipped learning. He instructed the rector, Dr. Mohamed Shaheen, to interview university professors and find out what they thought of flipped learning. Dr. Shaheen was instructed to simply present flipped learning and let the professors talk. By the end of the forum, approximately 80 percent of the profes-sors opposed flipped learning as a teaching methodology. Frustrated, Dr. Shaheen went to Dr. Arikan and asked for more direction. Dr. Arikan told him to repeat the forums and include students who attended the same universities at which the professors taught. The differences were stark. Eighty percent of the students wanted a flipped class experience. Student desires tipped the balance, and when MEF University opened its doors in 2014, it opened as the first fully flipped university in the world.

02

CHAPTER 2

THE HALLMARKS OF GOOD FLIPPED HOMEWORK

CREATING EFFECTIVE FLIPPED HOMEWORK ASSIGNMENTS

A flipped homework assignment usually takes the form of a short instructional video created by teachers and watched by students before class. It can also be a short interactive reading exercise with which students interact before class. The content of the prework depends on the class, the topic, and the level of the students. Prework is typically introductory in nature. For example, if a biology teacher created a video describing the function and timing of the different valves in the heart, the prework might be an in-class activity wherein students work with frog hearts. Another example: an elementary teacher creates a short video on identifying the main point in a reading and class time is devoted to students finding the main point in a different reading.

WHAT MAKES HOMEWORK EFFECTIVE

Cathy Vatterott (2010) identified five "hallmarks" of effective homework—purpose, efficiency, ownership, competence, and aesthetic appeal. Vatterott's work is the gold standard as regards the elements necessary for effective and meaningful homework. What strikes me about Vatterott's work is how flipped homework is an ideal medium for what she considers the hallmarks of effective homework. Let's examine each of the hallmarks in light of flipped homework and address how flipped homework is truly transforming the "H" word.

Purpose

Homework must have a specific purpose. If students view homework as meaningful, they are more likely to be engaged and to do the homework, and do it well. I believe that hardwired into all humans is a desire to learn. We are a curious species that thrives on input and feedback. Students are very perceptive. They can smell a mile away an assignment that has little to no purpose. Busywork is the death of purpose. Strive to make your homework meaningful.

In case you think I live in the world of non-reality, I want to acknowledge that not all homework will seem meaningful to every student. Not every student will love what we teach. Some kids may love math and dislike literature and vice versa. Learning is often hard, and some students want to take the easy way out. Not all of learning is, or should be, "fun." Sometimes students simply need to practice what they have learned in order to reinforce skills and knowledge. So don't get hung up on the issue of making homework entertaining. Rather, ensure that homework has purpose. All students, even those in a required class in which they are not interested, want to succeed.

Flipped videos are a way for students to access lower-level content so that class time is re-purposed for higher-order tasks and activities. Flipped homework assignments transform *class time* into time for *learning, engagement,* and *meaning.* Flipped learning makes homework more meaningful by making class time purposeful and engaging.

Efficiency

Most traditional homework takes too long. Students are often expected to work long hours after school on tasks they may not fully understand. As stated earlier, a flipped video, when done well, is short. In the student survey introduced in Chapter 1, I asked three questions related to how a flipped video addressed the efficiency issue:

1. *How much time does your flipped class homework take compared to the homework in your non-flipped classes?* It is interesting to note that while only 15 percent reported that it takes more time, most—52 percent—felt that a flipped homework assignment took less time (see Figure 2.1).

FIGURE 2.1
STUDENT RESPONSES REGARDING TIME FOR FLIPPED HOMEWORK VS. NON-FLIPPED HOMEWORK

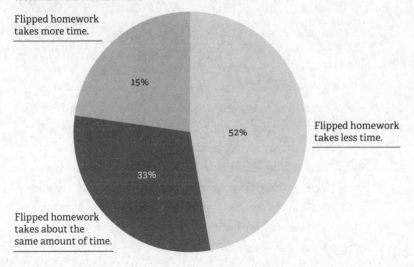

Flipped homework takes more time.

Flipped homework takes less time.

Flipped homework takes about the same amount of time.

15%

52%

33%

2. *When you watch a flipped video, how much total time does it take you to watch it, including the amount of time to pause and take notes?* The responses to this question (see Figure 2.2), coupled with those to the previous question, truly speak to the fact that homework takes less time and the amount of homework time can be predicted. This is huge. No longer do we need to worry that homework will take one student hours to complete and another minutes.

FIGURE 2.2
STUDENT RESPONSES REGARDING TIME TAKEN TO WATCH FLIPPED VIDEO

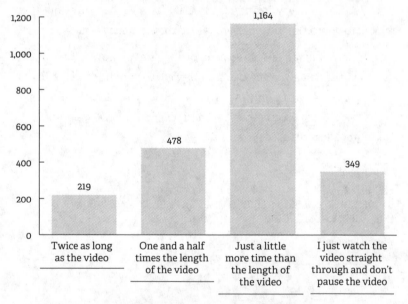

3. *On average, how many minutes are your teachers' flipped videos?* The magic of flipped learning does not happen on the video. Rather, the video sets up the classroom to be a place of rich learning and interaction. I am encouraged by student answers here (see Figure 2.3) because only a few of the students report excessively long flipped videos. Flipped videos should be short, dense sources of information. It is amazing how much content you can place in a short (micro) video.

FIGURE 2.3
STUDENT RESPONSES REGARDING LENGTH OF TEACHERS' FLIPPED VIDEOS

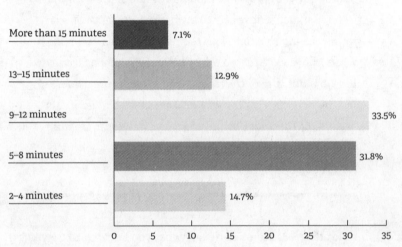

Ownership

In an ideal world, every student would love every class they take. They would be interested in every topic, be self-motivated, and would take complete ownership of their learning. However, for a variety of reasons, some students are not motivated in every class. How do we get buy-in from students? How do we get them to take ownership of their learning?

For those who are self-motivated by the topic, ownership is easy. The student who aspires to be a writer will enjoy writing, the student who likes to tinker will enjoy physics, and the student who loves storytelling will love history. But what about required courses that may leave some students undermotivated?

Relationship. I believe the key to getting ownership in any learning experience is a simple word: relationship. We as humans thrive best in the context of meaningful and positive relationships. We are hardwired to connect with other humans. One thing I have experienced and have heard countless times by flipped learning teachers is how it enhances relationships with students. Some time ago, Troy Faulkner, a high school math teacher in Minnesota, sent me this e-mail after the passing of his mother-in-law:

Thanks for your prayers. I thought I would share with you that my students have been showing empathy and concern for me during this time. I do not remember this occurring when I have experienced a loss before when I was lecturing. I am not sure of the reason why students are expressing their concern for my wife and me, but I wonder if it is because of the relationships that have developed because of me using flipped learning since I get to work with students one-on-one.

The old adage, "Students don't care what you know until they know that you care," rings true. If we want students to have ownership in our classes, we need to not reach just their heads, but also their hearts.

Engaging, relevant, and meaningful classes. Another aspect of getting students to take ownership in their learning is to make classes engaging, relevant, and meaningful. This is a complex problem, as each student comes to class with their own experiences and baggage. Flipped learning addresses this, as class time is re-imagined and there is time during class to create meaningful and enriching experiences. We teachers teach certain disciplines because, at some point in our lives, we were captured by the content. I taught chemistry because I had a love for science and a deep appreciation of the natural world. The last thing I wanted to do was to turn my students off from something I loved.

And when I got away from whole-class dissemination of knowledge and created a class that expressed the richness of science, the vast majority of my students had a greater appreciation for chemistry. I saw them talking about chemistry in the halls, helping each other with difficult concepts, and that they were genuinely engaged in class. At the end of each school year, I had students do a summative project. I designed the project such that it connected most of the topics about which students learned throughout the year. I gave them a one-page explanation of the project and three weeks of class time to complete it. They demonstrated their work by turning in an extended paper, which was usually around 40 pages long. Secondly, I interviewed each student, at which time I asked higher-order conceptual questions that got to the heart of the course. I had designed the project before I began flipping my classes and saw remarkable differences once the class format changed. I noticed the greatest differences during the interviews, in which students were able to interact with me on a much deeper level. The questions I asked went further and, for the most part, became more of a conversation about chemistry and less of a focused question-and-answer session. I credit flipped learning with this transformation. The students embraced the hard work and messiness of learning and took ownership of their learning.

Choice. I believe that giving students choice will increase their ownership of their learning (see Figure 2.4). I believe in curriculum and content, but if we want to get buy-in from our students, let's give them some choice in their learning. Many smart people have sat on curriculum committees and decided what is important for students to learn. These meetings have resulted in our current standards and expectations. I agree that in our society there are things we should expect all students to learn and be able to do. But my argument here is that we need to give students some choice in their learning, which will result in increased

FIGURE 2.4
CONTENT VS. STUDENT CHOICE

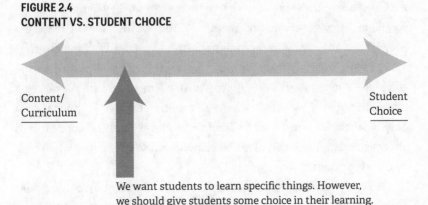

Content/
Curriculum

Student
Choice

We want students to learn specific things. However, we should give students some choice in their learning.

student ownership of learning. Students' interests may lie outside of the set standards and competencies. I like to think of it as a continuum, where on one side is content and standards and on the other is choice.

While the vast majority of my students chose to watch and interact with my flipped video, some students chose to access the content in other ways. Examples of choice I have seen used include:

- Allowing students to watch the teacher-created video or an online video.
- Allowing students to read the textbook instead of the flipped video.
- Allowing students to engage in an online simulation instead of the teacher-created video.
- Allowing students to choose how they interact with the content (e.g., some students need the structure of a notes handout while others can simply watch a video for understanding).

Ultimately, it is important to know the strengths and weaknesses of individual students to determine the best way for them to access and interact with flipped homework.

Competence

Too often, homework is simply too hard for students. We teachers complain that students do not do our homework and often it is because we are sending them home with assignments that they simply cannot complete. They get home and might try but, for a variety of reasons, they have neither the background nor the expertise to complete the assignment. However, a flipped video is something that all students can complete. When done well, a flipped video will focus on lower-level cognition. In terms of Bloom's Taxonomy, I recommend that a flipped video only be at the knowledge or understanding level. Save the application, analysis, and higher-level cognition components for class time, when the teacher is present.

Recently my daughter's friend, who is in a flipped math class at her high school, told me that she loved the flipped classroom model. I asked her why and she said: "I finally get math." I pressed her for a deeper explanation, and she told me that the homework was easy and, better yet, she had all of class time to get help from her teacher on the things she didn't understand.

In the student survey that I referenced in Chapter 1, I asked students, "How do flipped videos help students understand class content?" I asked them to use a scale of 1 to 5, with 1 being flipped videos make understanding much harder and 5 being flipped videos make understanding much easier. As shown in Figure 2.5, the vast majority felt that flipped videos were a great help.

FIGURE 2.5
STUDENT RESPONSES REGARDING FLIPPED VIDEOS AND UNDERSTANDING CONTENT
(with 1 being "Make understanding much harder" and 5 being "Make understanding much easier")

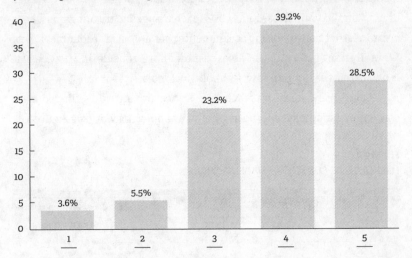

Aesthetic Appeal

As I read the research on the hallmarks of good homework, I was particularly surprised by the inclusion of aesthetic appeal. What an assignment looks like really makes a difference to students. Magdalen Radovich, who we met in Chapter 1, told me that her teachers, when they moved to the flipped class model, "upped" their game. Instead of sending busy and often meaningless work home, her teachers started to improve the quality and *look* of the homework. I believe this is because a flipped video is a very public learning object; it will be accessed by students, parents, and possibly countless others. In my case, when I posted my instructional videos on YouTube and started receiving comments from all over the world, I was motivated to create quality content.

Magdalen also noted that when teachers coupled their flipped videos with a formative tool such as a Google Forms, the clean design simply looked good. She notes that many of her non-flipped staff often send home poorly designed homework that is unappealing and looks like it was thrown together at the last moment, and students notice this. Now that so many quality learning objects are easily available, today's media-savvy students have higher expectations. Regardless of whether or not you flip your classroom, we as teachers need to up our games. Let's create aesthetically pleasing assignments that enhance student learning. We really don't have much of an excuse anymore, considering how easy it is now to access high-quality technological tools.

Manel Trenchs, an art teacher in France, organizes his flipped class content in a simple, clean, and aesthetically appealing way (see Figure 2.6).

FIGURE 2.6
FLIPPED CLASS CONTENT OF MANEL TRENCHS

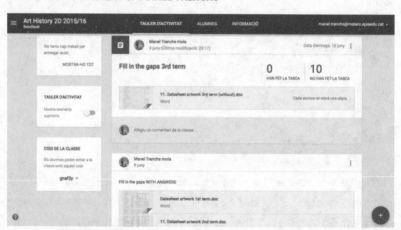

Flipped homework represents a paradigm shift in homework design, while at the same time representing the best aspects of what makes homework effective. In the next chapter, we will look at practical strategies for creating meaningful homework in a flipped context.

03

CHAPTER 3

FLIPPED STRATEGIES FOR EDUCATORS

Flipping a class is not for the faint of heart. It requires a rethinking of both homework and class time. It presents new challenges that teachers must master. This chapter focuses on the unique strategies needed to make the entire flipped class experience a success for both students and teachers.

HELP! MY KIDS DIDN'T DO THE HOMEWORK

Let's just say it: not all students will do homework. Homework completion is a problem that occurs whether or not you flip your class. I had students who did not complete flipped homework, so flipped videos are not the magic bullet to solve the homework completion problem. But I can say that a greater percentage of students completed flipped video assignments than did traditional homework assignments. Here are some practical suggestions that will increase the chances that students will complete a flipped video assignment.

Make Students Accountable

Students need to know that they will be held accountable for the work that they do. One way to hold students accountable is to assign a grade to watching the video. Students who don't comply are then required to watch the flipped videos in class while the students who completed the assignment apply the concepts in the flipped video and essentially do the "hard stuff." Those students who did not complete the flipped video assignment will quickly learn that, in the long run, it is easier and less time-consuming for them to complete the homework.

Get Help from Your Students' Peers

Design a class activity that can only be completed if *all* students complete the prework. In such a situation, peer pressure is often placed on those who did not complete the requisite work. During a trip to the United Kingdom, I chatted with some students in a flipped class about those students who did not do the flipped homework. They told me that when a peer did not hold up their end of the bargain, they would "get on their case" because they had to pick up their "slack."

Call Home

Call home and discuss with parents why their child is not being successful in your class. When I chatted with parents and explained the nature of a flipped video assignment, they were very supportive.

Chat with Students Individually

Chat one-on-one with a student who is not watching a flipped video and find out what is going on. In many instances, simply pointing out how necessary flipped assignments are to their success in the classroom will get students on track. I believe that most students want to do well.

They are sometimes just so overwhelmed with their lives that school sometimes takes a back seat. And having a listening ear goes a long way toward student success.

I often discovered during one-on-one conversations with my students that there were issues (such as after-school jobs or family issues) that prevented them from completing homework assignments. In one case, I noticed a student who was struggling greatly and, through my interactions with him, I learned that he had become homeless. I then connected him with some of the mental health professionals in our school, and he was able to get the help he needed. If this student had been in my traditional (that is, non-flipped) class, I'm not sure that I would have spotted his signs of distress and gotten him the help he needed. Problems such as these existed before I flipped my class, but after I flipped my class, I began to notice them more because of my increased interactions with students. The deeper interactions reinforced for me the importance of relationships in education.

Don't Rescue Kids

Many teachers make the mistake of "bailing out" students who did not watch the flipped video by providing those students with live instruction. This sends the message to students who completed the assignments that doing so is not worthwhile. Never rescue students for poor choices.

Make Class More Engaging

Kids really want to learn. And the more engaging and relevant the in-class experiences, the more students will buy into the class and want to do the prework. Thus, designing an engaging class is key to making the flipped class work.

CREATING QUALITY FLIPPED VIDEOS

The vast majority of teachers who flip their classes leverage video for the prework. Following are best practices for creating *effective* flipped videos:

- *Short.* A flipped video, when done well, is short. For elementary students, the videos should be less than 10 minutes in length, and for secondary students, less than 15 minutes in length. Flipped videos should also be very focused on a particular learning objective. A seven-minute-long video should take a student roughly 10 to 15 minutes to complete (as the student will be interacting by taking notes, answering questions, asking questions, pausing, and rewinding).

- *One topic.* Each flipped video should cover one topic. If a lesson has multiple parts, it is best to create multiple videos to address the topic.

- *Interactive.* It is imperative that students don't just watch the video; they should be required to *do something* with it. Have students take notes, answer questions, or respond to a prompt in an online tool. (The myriad ways to build interactivity into a flipped video will be discussed in detail later in the book.)

- *Introductory.* Flipped videos typically introduce new material that is then delved into deeply during class time. However, some teachers flip the flipped video concept and create flipped videos that are used in the middle of the instructional cycle rather than at the beginning. This is particularly the case when teachers are using an inquiry process.

For many teachers, video is a new teaching medium. Following are some best practices for creating *engaging* flipped videos:

- *Keep text to a minimum.* Teachers often make the mistake of creating text-heavy flipped videos. Video is a visual medium and is best suited for images and action. Don't simply make a video of a busy PowerPoint slide. If students need to read something, then assign a reading. I have found that, in many cases, replacing a teacher's PowerPoint slide with a great graphic and then using the text as the script for the video works very well.

- *Don't go it alone.* Include a teacher-partner in the video. One teacher should play the role of the expert and the other the role of an inquisitive student. Students will find this person-to-person interaction engaging, and they will retain more of the information relayed.

- *Pay particular attention to audio quality.* The one overlooked technical detail about flipped videos is the quality of the audio. The microphone in most modern devices is usually adequate. However, it is important that the recording takes place in a quiet room.

- *Include annotations.* Drawing on the screen using a pen input device will significantly increase the level of student engagement. There are a variety of ways to annotate—apps, external writing pads, or a recording of a teacher standing at a whiteboard are three examples.

- *Animate your voice.* Some teachers clam up when making a video without a live audience. While it may not be easy to talk with energy and enthusiasm when recording a video in a room by yourself, you must keep in mind the audience you are trying to engage—your students. When recording, speak as if the students are actually there. Add humor, creativity, and fun to your flipped videos.

Additionally, a video checklist is provided in the Appendix at the end of this book. The checklist, which includes 17 items to consider when creating a quality video, is divided into three parts—technology considerations, video content, and other considerations.

TEACH YOUR STUDENTS HOW TO WATCH FLIPPED VIDEOS

Watching an instructional video is different than watching a video for entertainment. Students inherently understand how to watch the latest superhero movie, but they need to be taught how to watch instructional content. I liken the difference to learning to read a textbook rather than a novel. This is a skill that must be taught. Teachers should spend some time at the beginning of the school year teaching their students how to watch instructional video content. Ross Nelson, a 6th grade mathematics teacher in Texas, has an effective way he teaches this process. He spends the first two to three weeks of school watching the videos with his students in class and guides his students through the following three steps to ensure that they are learning from the video:

1. *Watch, listen, and process.* Students watch, listen to, and process the information in the video.

2. *Pause and write.* Students then pause and write down what they've seen in the video. This ensures that students have another opportunity to process what they've just seen as they take notes on the video. In addition, they now have a record of their learning to which to refer during in-class practice.

3. *Accountability.* Lastly, students answer a five-question formative assessment. Those students who meet the minimum threshold of 80 percent and present their notes move on to the daily assignment. Students who do not meet the minimum must attend a small-group tutorial session led by Mr. Nelson.

As a high school teacher, I spent the first few days of class teaching students how to interact with instructional videos. My approach was similar to Nelson's. However, because my students were more mature that those taught by Nelson, I spent a minimal amount of time teaching this skill. One key thing I made sure my students worked on, as did Nelson, was to emphasize the need for a distraction-free setting for flipped video homework (as it is difficult for students to learn while simultaneously spending time on Instagram, texting, or and watching TV). The time spent teaching students how to watch and interact with instructional content will pay great dividends in helping them become self-directed learners.

DON'T ASSIGN VIDEO HOMEWORK AND SOMETHING ELSE

One mistake some teachers make is to use the flipped class to increase the workload of students. Teachers assign a video *and* traditional homework. My experience has been that this will derail the flipped classroom model. I highly discourage teachers from using the flipped class to increase the workload of students and impinge on students' home time. Using a flipped video as homework brings value to homework time by introducing content rather than expecting students to apply and analyze content in a vacuum. If video is being used to flip a class, it should *replace* work a teacher would have previously sent home—*not add to it.* Some students in the survey cited in Chapter 1 stated that they viewed flipped video assignments as additional assignments, not as replacement assignments.

MAKING INTERACTIVE VIDEOS

My goal is not for students to watch a video. My goal is for students to *interact* with content, which then sets them up for a more engaging class experience. It is important to create systems that encourage student interactions. Following are strategies that teachers may use to increase the interactivity of flipped videos:

- *Advanced organizers.* These could be as simple as a fill-in-the-blank "guided notes sheet," a template for Cornell-style notes, or a page with all of the necessary charts and problems with a QR (quick response) code to direct students to the online video.
- *3-2-1 strategy.* Students record *three* things they learned from the video, *two* questions about the content from the video, and *one* lingering question. During class, students report the three things they learned, interact with each other about the two questions, and share with their teacher the one point they did not understand. Students who feel that they completely grasped the content record a takeaway that summarizes their learning.

There is no one way to build in interactivity. And there is no one tool that is best for every teacher. Finding what works best in any class depends on many factors, and each teacher must find the right mix of interactive techniques, tools, and systems.

CREATION VS. CURATION

Who should make the flipped videos? Should teachers find resources online or create their own? Though I don't have hard research on this issue, I have heard from teachers that when they create their own video content, there is an increase in student engagement and attention. Teacher-created videos are more effective because teaching is inherently about human interaction. Students neither know nor associate with the person who created an online video. Teachers know their students best. One teacher summed it up at a recent conference when he said, "I could spend hours and hours looking for the perfect video on YouTube or I could just make it myself." This is not to say that you should never use outside resources, but the default should be for the teacher to be the primary creator of the content.

ALTERNATIVE HOMEWORK ASSIGNMENTS

Though this book is primarily about how flipped learning can solve the homework problem, a flipped video is not the only way to make homework meaningful for students. One technique I am particularly fond of is Teachers Involve Parents in Schoolwork—TIPS. TIPS is a project that has proven to make homework effective by getting students to involve their parents in the homework experience.

As a science teacher, I have assigned experiments for students to do at home based on the work of my former colleague Mark Paricio—an award-winning science teacher at Smokey Hill High School in Aurora, Colorado. Mark designed simple experiments students could perform at home using simple household items. Mark realized that people learn best when they have to teach others. Thus the expectation was that students would conduct home experiments and explain the results to their parents. Not only did these help students to have rich experiences, it had the side benefit of involving parents in their children's education. I got more thank-you letters from parents of students to whom I assigned take-home labs than I did for any other types of assignments.

Another example of a TIPS assignment comes from the TIPS Manual for Teachers (Epstein, Davis, Logan, Moore, Myers, Cole, Hammonds & Taylor, 1992). The assignment involves having students ask parents about the hairstyles that were popular when they were children, and whether the hairstyle was approved by the older generation and why. The assignment is designed to have students write a compare-and-contrast paper.

For more examples of or to learn more about TIPS assignments, go to http://files.eric.ed.gov/fulltext/ED355032.pdf.

EXTEND THE LEARNING TO HOME

Students need to see how what they learn in school applies to their everyday lives. Connecting differing aspects of life together can be very powerful for students. For example, in a primary classroom, a teacher might have students write down words at home that start with the letter of a given day of the week. Or a teacher might have students take pictures of objects that have the shape about which they are learning in school. Although such assignments fall into the application level of Bloom's Taxonomy, they are certainly achievable for the vast majority of students.

MAKING CLASS TIME MORE MEANINGFUL

While this is a book on homework, not classwork, I feel that if you want to increase the value of homework, the most important thing you can do is to increase the levels of engagement and interaction in the classroom. So you created your video, assigned it, and had students interact with it. Great. Now, what do you do in class? This is not an easy questions to answer, because what a high school English teacher would do in the classroom versus what an elementary art teacher would do in the classroom differs greatly. My best advice on this topic is to respond with a question: what is the best use of your face-to-face class time?

Let's look at a few strategies that I see teachers using *during* class once they have assigned a flipped video as homework.

Peer Instruction

Peer instruction is a learning system designed by Eric Mazur, a physics professor at Harvard University (Mazur, 1996). Mazur was dissatisfied with the traditional lecture format and wanted his students to have in-depth understanding of the concepts he teaches. His students learn rudimentary concepts at home and, during class, Mazur takes them through the peer instruction cycle, which comprises the following steps:

1. Instructor poses question based on students' responses to their pre-class reading.
2. Students reflect on the question.
3. Students commit to an individual answer.
4. Instructor reviews student responses.
5. Students discuss their thinking and answers with their peers.
6. Students then commit again to an individual answer.
7. The instructor again reviews responses and decides whether more explanation is needed before moving on to the next concept.

A good peer-instruction exercise involves having higher-order thinking problems with which students struggle together in class. This method has a mixture of individual accountability and group work, which helps students engage and learn deeply. To learn more about peer instruction, I encourage you to read Dr. Mazur's book *Peer Instruction: A User's Manual* (Addison Wesley, 1996).

Genius Hour

One of the exciting things we are seeing flipped classroom teachers adopt is the genius hour approach. The idea behind genius hour—sometimes called *passion projects* or *20 percent time*—can be traced to a practice employed by companies such as Google. In this approach, employees are allowed to use a portion of their working hours to work on projects about which they are passionate. When applied to a classroom, teachers are devoting some of the recovered class time from flipped learning to passion projects. A typical flipped learning teacher who teaches five classes a week would teach using a flipped approach for four days a week and then give students one day a week to work on passion projects.

I have been amazed at the creativity and excitement evident when I have been in flipped classes where the teacher is implementing genius hour. I have seen students design cars, create a ferro-fluid, design fuel cells, write original music, write short stories, research the human brain, and so on. Student curiosity and interest is something that is missing in the test-driven culture in which many teachers exist. To learn more about genius hour and to get practical advice about implementation, go to http://www.20timeineducation.com/20-time-ideas.

Projects and Project-Based Learning

Teachers recognize that larger-scale projects are powerful tools for student growth. The open-ended nature of projects allows students to dive deeper into some aspect of their learning and allows for greater creativity and engagement. However, projects are time-consuming. If a teacher gives up valuable class time for projects, parts of the curriculum will likely get left out. And in this age of high-stakes tests and accountability, some teachers have chosen to do fewer projects in class. The beauty of flipped learning is that it gives teachers more time in class to do projects.

Teachers have always had students doing projects. Project-based learning (PBL), however, is something different. It was best explained to me by John Mergendoller, the former executive director of the Buck Institute for Education, the leading project-based organization in the world. John said that in most schools, projects are the dessert, but that in true PBL, the project is the main course. What often happens in PBL classes that are flipped is that the flipped videos are not shown first. Instead, students work on the project at hand and then the videos are accessible for them when they need it. Thus, the video is in the middle, not at the beginning, of the learning cycle.

Mastery/Competency-Based Education

I believe one of the best ways to teach is through mastery. The mastery movement has recently gained steam and is now re-branded as competency-based education. The main tenants of competency-based education are:

- Students advance upon demonstrated mastery.
- Competencies include explicit, measurable, transferable learning objectives that empower students.
- Assessment is meaningful and a positive learning experience for students.
- Students receive rapid, differentiated support based on their individual learning needs.
- Learning outcomes emphasize competencies that include application and creation of knowledge along with the development of important skills and dispositions.

As I see it, mastery based education has two huge logistical challenges:

1. *Finding the right time for direct instruction.* Since direct instruction is often given to a large group of students at the same time, this makes mastery difficult. Students who have not mastered content get information early, and those who have are bored.
2. *Assessment.* In a true mastery system, it's difficult to manage students who are taking assessments at different times.

In 2008, Aaron Sams and I developed what we called the flipped-mastery model, which addresses these two challenges. In the case of direct instruction, the flipped videos can be watched when each student is ready for the content. And the assessment issue is solved using testing software that is now available to all.

Flipped mastery was the single best thing I ever did in education. It is a way to manage a true mastery system and provide individual feedback for students, give them the challenges they need, differentiate for each student, and provide appropriate feedback for all students. For details about flipped mastery, read *Flip Your Classroom: Reach Every Student in Every Class Every Day* (Bergmann & Sams, 2012).

04

CHAPTER 4

ASSESSING AND GRADING FLIPPED HOMEWORK

Since flipped homework is a paradigm shift in what effective homework should look like, how a teacher assesses and grades flipped homework will require rethinking.

Flipped learning revolutionized the way that I thought about assessment. For my first 19 years as a teacher, I taught traditionally and used traditional assessment and grading policies. I lectured, had students take notes and do experiments, and, at the end of each unit, gave students a paper-and-pencil test. I graded on a percentage scale: students who got above 90 percent got an A and those who got below 60 percent failed. However, when I helped pioneer flipped learning, things began to change. First, I realized that the model hinged on students watching the flipped videos at home. Second, it became apparent that many students were watching, but not successfully learning from, the flipped videos. Next, I began to rethink formative assessment. And lastly, I realized I needed to rethink my grading policies.

Interaction was the guiding theme throughout my transformation. I needed students to meaningfully interact with content in a way that set them up for success in the classroom. This chapter will focus on strategies that enable teachers to have greater access to formative data, to use that data to differentiate, and to grade in a way commensurate with the unique nature of teaching in a flipped classroom environment.

ACCOUNTABILITY

Before flipping my class, students took notes, which I rarely graded, during my lectures. I assumed that if they were taking notes, then they were engaged and learning. However, since the flipped class model hinged on students doing the prework, I felt there was a need to determine if they watched the video. At first, I looked for technological solutions that would ensure that students viewed the video. But it was 2007, and technological tracking tools were not very accessible. So, as students walked into class, I simply checked their notes and assigned points. However, this had an unintended consequence in that the number of gradebook entries doubled. The extra entries were worth it, as this kept students accountable for watching the flipped videos. Since that time, I visited countless teachers around the globe, and many of them do not check each student's entry each day. They put the ownership of the prework on the students and expect them to get it done. My recommendation is that you determine what works best for your students. Will the majority of them be responsible if you do not have a built-in system to check, or do they need the added accountability? I personally feel that, in most cases, teachers should check students' flipped homework. However, I have seen some instances where students do not need that level of accountability.

TECH TOOLS FOR ACCOUNTABILITY AND INTERACTIVITY

With the growth of both the flipped model and technological advancements, students can now interact with and give feedback on videos through a variety of online tools—some that collect information after students watch a video and others that gather information while the video is being viewed. Tools such as Google Forms, online assessment suites, and most learning management systems have quizzing features that allow the teacher to get immediate feedback on learning. These tools are usually in the form of a short quiz or questionnaire to which students respond after watching the video. Though they do not track the time students spend watching the video, many teachers find these tools very useful for getting formative feedback on student comprehension and engagement.

Rebekah Cerqua, a chemistry teacher in Indiana, uses Google Forms to determine the degree of understanding of the information presented in the flipped video (see Figure 4.1). The data from Rebekah's questionnaire then flow into a self-grading spreadsheet from which she gets instant feedback on student comprehension (see Figure 4.2).

Many new online educational services—for example, EDpuzzle, Microsoft Office Mix, and PlayPosit—contain tools that allow teachers to embed questions within the flipped video. When this is done, the video will pause and students are asked to respond to a question or prompt.

FIGURE 4.1
QUESTIONNAIRE TO DETERMINE DEGREE OF UNDERSTANDING

Which is the best option for the meaning of "p" in pH?
- ○ positive
- ○ power
- ○ reference solution

H+ ions are also known as
- ○ electrons
- ○ neutrons
- ○ protons

Define pH in your OWN words

Short answer text

Water can function as both as acid and base.
- ○ True
- ○ False

FIGURE 4.2
SELF-GRADING SPREADSHEET

	A	C	D	H	I	O	P
2	**Summary:**						
3	4	*Points Possible*	4	*Average Points*	3.60	*Counted Submissions*	24
5	**Name**	**Total Points**	**Percent**	**Question 1**	**Question 2**	**Question 3**	**Question 4**
14		3	75.00%	1	0	1	1
15		3	75.00%	0	1	1	1
16		4	100.00%	1	1	1	1
17		4	100.00%	1	1	1	1
18		4	100.00%	1	1	1	1
19		3	75.00%	0	1	1	1
20		4	100.00%	1	1	1	1
21		3	75.00%	0	1	1	1
22		4	100.00%	1	1	0	0

Student Submissions | Grades

Such services have analytics that enable teachers to determine which students watched the video, for how long each student watched the video, and which questions were answered correctly, as well as provide discussion forums about the video.

Figure 4.3, a screenshot from EDpuzzle, contains the names of the students who completed the flipped video and the grades they received on the embedded questions.

FIGURE 4.3
NAMES AND GRADES OF STUDENTS WHO COMPLETED THE FLIPPED VIDEO

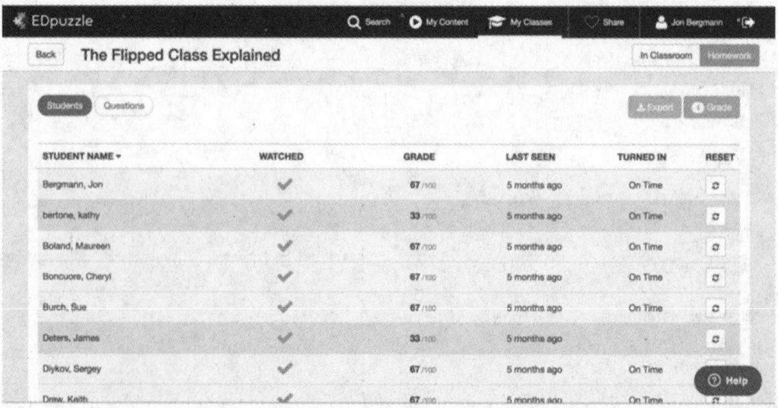

STUDENT NAME	WATCHED	GRADE	LAST SEEN	TURNED IN	RESET
Bergmann, Jon	✓	67 /100	5 months ago	On Time	
bertone, kathy	✓	33 /100	5 months ago	On Time	
Boland, Maureen	✓	67 /100	5 months ago	On Time	
Boncuore, Cheryl	✓	67 /100	5 months ago	On Time	
Burch, Sue	✓	67 /100	5 months ago	On Time	
Deters, James	✓	33 /100	5 months ago	-	
Diykov, Sergey	✓	67 /100	5 months ago	On Time	
Drew, Keith	✓	67 /100	5 months ago	On Time	

ADVANCED ORGANIZERS

Many teachers create advanced organizers that students must complete as they interact with the flipped videos (as some students need the additional structure to help them comprehend the content). As relevant diagrams and charts can be placed into the organizer, when students use advanced organizers when watching flipped videos, the amount of time it takes to interact with the video is shortened. As well, advanced organizers allow teachers to more rapidly evaluate the quality of students' notes (as the format is uniform). On the flip side, advanced organizers force students to interact with the flipped video in a specific way—which is beneficial for students who need structure and inhibiting for those who don't.

Ultimately, teachers need to evaluate their students, their content, and their teaching style to determine if advanced organizers are something that will be beneficial for their students. I found that the vast majority of my students responded well to the advanced organizers, and allowed those who found them restrictive to interact with the videos in other ways (some simply watched the video; others took notes in their own manner; and yet others wanted to have a short, individual or small group conversation with me about the content).

Rebekah Cerqua's students use advanced organizers, with a QR code that links the organizer to the corresponding flipped videos (see Figure 4.4).

SUMMARY SHEETS

Nicholas Bennett, a math teacher in Virginia, requires his students to both take notes and fill out a summary sheet (see Figure 4.5) after viewing each flipped video. Organizers such as this help students process what they learn and help teachers keep track of understanding.

PAPER OR DIGITAL?

When taking notes on a flipped video, should a student take notes on paper or should they take notes digitally? A recent study investigated the

FIGURE 4.4
ADVANCED ORGANIZER WITH QR CODE

16.1 Solutions Lecture Notes

Directions
1. Watch the lecture.
2. As you watch the lecture, complete this worksheet.
3. Then complete the Google Form, "16.1 Lecture response."

16.1 Properties of Solutions
Factors that affect how a substance dissolves

1. _____
2. _____
3. _____

Define solubility

Explain the difference between a solute and a solvent

FIGURE 4.5
SUMMARY SHEET

Name:_____ Date:_____ Period:_____

	Video Title:_____	Video duration: _____:_____
Monday	Summary:_____	
	_____	Parent/Guardian Signature:
	_____	
	_____	
	Was the video helpful: Yes / No If not, explain:	(sign above line)
	_____	Score: _____/_____

performance of paper note-takers versus digital note-takers (Mueller & Oppenheimer, 2014). In the study, all of the students watched a TED video, and half of the students took notes on paper while the other half took notes on a laptop computer. Students who took notes on a laptop tended to record verbatim the content of the lecture (which researchers theorized was because students can type faster than they can write). Students who took notes on paper wrote less and had to conceptualize the content. The students then took a short exam about what they had learned. The exam results revealed a notable difference between the those who took notes on the laptop computer versus those who took notes on paper: while there was little difference between the scores when students were asked questions pertaining to the facts, paper note-takers scored significantly higher when asked conceptual-application questions.

Beth Holland (2014), who took issue with the study, believes that students need to be taught how to take adequate digital notes. She contends that digital notes have the following advantages over paper notes:

- Allow for easier searching
- Are easier to share
- Help students with executive functioning challenges. How many students lose the papers on which they write their notes? Also, the study measured college students, not 7th graders.

So which is it? Should students interact with flipped videos on paper or digitally? My recommendation is that all teachers utilize digital tools that track student viewership that intersperse questions within the video, thereby giving teachers real-time information about student comprehension and enabling better differentiation of in-class activities. But this is still inadequate. Students still need a place where they process information in a meaningful way. For many, paper notes are the only option, as many students may not have access to a device on which to take adequate digital notes. But for those schools with a more robust technological infrastructure, digital notes can be advantageous if students are taught how to take sound digital notes.

CHECK FOR UNDERSTANDING WITH FLIPPED VIDEO QUESTIONS

It is best practice to embed questions into a video using one of the tech tools mentioned previously. But how often and what types of questions should be asked? Let us recall that the key to an effective flipped video is that it is introductory in nature. From a Bloom's Taxonomic perspective, the video teaches at a knowledge or understanding level. Thus, the majority of the embedded questions should be focused on checking for understanding. The student responses can inform instruction and differentiation.

I believe that a flipped video should, toward the end, include either an open-ended question (for example, "What do you wonder about?" "What don't you understand?" "How is the content of the video connected to x?") or a question that takes students deeper. Christopher Brady and James Plaza, both of whom teach social studies in Illinois, end their videos with a question. After watching a video about the causes of World War I, they asked students to ponder the question, "Why did the United States enter World War I?" They ask this in the video to set up class time, the focus of which will be to discuss the deeper question, and having students come to class with some starting ideas has proven to be a catalyst for richer discussions.

FORMATIVE DATA INFORMS INSTRUCTION AND DIFFERENTIATION

One of the benefits of collecting digital data from flipped videos is how the data inform teachers about student understanding. This data is a powerful tool for instruction. When I taught traditionally, I often asked the entire class about their comprehension, and the feedback was often inconsistent. Some students clearly understood the topic, others floundered, and yet others communicated to me that they understood, when in fact they had profound misconceptions. But now with the personalized tools available, teachers can know, and can easily access, relevant data on each student. And the beauty is that teachers know this information before students walk into class. Once a teacher has this information, he can aid student comprehension in the following ways:

- *Teachers can help struggling students.* When a teacher discovers gaps in understanding, she can target those students who need extra support.
- *Teachers can target fundamental misconceptions.* Often questions answered incorrectly indicate where student gaps occur.
- *Teachers can know which students can move on.* Have you ever taught something that the vast majority of your students already understand? If you find out from your flipped video data that all of your students get it, then don't waste time re-teaching.

The data, in addition to informing instruction, inform differentiation. Russ Trible, a 6th grade math teacher in Texas, requires his to students watch a short video, take notes in an advanced organizer, and then answer a few questions in a Google Form. Before class, he evaluates student responses and then puts students into two groups. Students who score 80 percent or higher are instructed to begin the in-class activity right away, and those with lower scores get a mini-tutorial. During the tutorial, students can practice, get clarification, and receive direct instruction (which is usually all his students need to begin the in-class activity). When I observed his class, approximately seven of his 30 students needed additional assistance, and this enabled him to meet the needs of both the struggling students and those who were ready to participate right away.

EVALUATE STUDENT UNDERSTANDING BY HAVING STUDENTS LEAD THE CLASS

I recently visited Kirk Humphries' 7th grade flipped math class in Deerfield, Illinois, and was impressed with how he started his flipped class. Most flipped class teachers begin the class by either answering questions from the flipped video or by giving students a short quiz, neither of which Kirk did. Instead, Kirk asked students to summarize the video. He sat in the back of the class and let the students take charge. The first student got up and grabbed a whiteboard marker and discussed what he learned. After a short time, another student raised his hand. The first student tossed the marker to the second student, who began to share. Then another student asked a question. The whole class turned to Mr. Humphries and hoped he would answer. Instead, Kirk threw the question back to the class and asked the students if any of them had an idea about how to answer their classmate's question. Up jumped another student, who took the lead and helped out the student with the question. For ten minutes, I sat in amazement at how well a group of 13-year-old students discussed math. It was magical. Students were taking ownership of their learning and were processing the content together. Kirk only intervened when necessary.

ENCOURAGING CURIOSITY THROUGH STUDENT-GENERATED QUESTIONS

As a science teacher, I sought to encourage my students to marvel at the natural world. The universe, from the smallest particle to the largest galaxy, is wondrous and beautiful. Students are naturally curious, and schools should tap into this fundamental drive. One way I evaluated student understanding from flipped videos was to have students include a question in their flipped video notes. The question had to be one to which they did not know the answer, and I encouraged students to write questions that sparked wonder and exploration.

During class time, each student spent a couple minutes with me, either in a small group or individually. During our brief conversations, students would first show me their completed notes (accountability) and then they asked me their questions. This may have been the single most rewarding activity I did with students for the following reasons:

- *Every student asks a question.* When I taught class the traditional way, only a select few students engaged with questions.

But when every student had a private audience with me, the nature and substance of the questioning went to a new level.

- *Questions expose gaps and misconceptions.* Student questions often revealed gaps in understanding and misconceptions. Before I encouraged student-generated questions, gaps and misconceptions were often difficult to determine (in many cases, students think they know something, when in fact they don't). The daily, private interactions with students allowed me to quickly close the gaps and clear up misconceptions.

Teaching students how to ask quality questions from the flipped videos was sometimes a challenge. I recall one young lady who only asked questions about topics that were clearly covered in the video. She struggled to take her questions deeper and enter the realms of wonder and curiosity. However, as she asked me questions almost every day, she progressed and, by the end of the year, had progressed significantly.

GRADING

If you want to get into an argument with teachers, discuss grading policies. Grading is one of the most contentious issues in education. Some teachers believe in a strict point system, and others in standards-based grading. Some will not accept late assignments, while others give students leeway. How do flipped homework assignments change grading policies and systems?

In many ways, grading policies do not have to change when flipped homework assignments are given. Flipped homework can be assigned points and graded like any other assignment. When I first flipped my class in 2007, I assigned 10 points to each video and dutifully recorded them in the gradebook. I was a stickler for keeping track of everything a student turned in, penalized those who turned in late assignments, and pursued kids who fell behind. But then something began to change in me. I began to see learning more holistically. I saw students as needing something more personalized and directed. I then read articles about the problems with percentage grading systems. In *Phi Delta Kappan*, an article by Douglas Reeves (2004) convinced me that giving students a zero on an assignment hurts students. And then as I pioneered the flipped-mastery model, I gravitated toward a standards-based grading system. In my interactions with countless flipped class teachers around the globe, I have seen a similar transformation. Most of them start out with traditional grading systems and paradigms, but as they master the flipped class method and embrace it as more of a philosophy rather than a technique, their grading practices evolve. They see learning, not grading and marking, as the goal of education. So it is OK to use traditional grading systems with flipped learning, but I want to push those who, like me, were stuck in the old paradigm. Keep in the back of your mind that as you progress down the path of flipped learning, you, too, will begin to rethink traditional grading policies.

STUDENT ASSESSMENT OF YOUR FLIPPED CLASS

It is useful to periodically poll your students about their perceptions, frustrations, and ideas about the flipped class you have set up. Not surprisingly, students often provide the best feedback and their input will help you become a better teacher. I frequently asked my students to tell me what they liked and disliked about flipped learning. For example, when I first put the webcam into the screencasting video, students told me they liked it because I was no longer a disembodied voice—I was their teacher. My students also gave me great suggestions about how to better assess them, how to better organize the content, and how to better utilize some of the aspects of my learning management system. I collected their responses by simply asking them for feedback as I was working with them and also through a survey that I gave to students at the end of each semester. The sample survey in the Appendix can be used as a guide to help you create your own survey.

05

CHAPTER 5
STRATEGIES FOR SCHOOLS, ADMINISTRATORS, AND PARENTS

Homework is not just a struggle for teachers and students; it impacts parents, administrators, and the entire school climate. Having individual teachers flipping their classes and making homework more meaningful and effective is good, but how do we scale flipped learning? How should a school involve parents, and how can leadership model flipped learning? What systems need to be in place in order for flipped learning to have maximum impact?

CRAFTING A NEW TYPE OF HOMEWORK POLICY

I have served on the homework committee of the schools in which I've worked. At one of the schools, I recall one painful meeting whose goal was to determine the number of minutes of homework for each child at each grade level and in each subject. The meeting was contentious, as teachers tried to justify why they should be allowed to assign more homework than other teachers. At the end of the meeting, each subject and grade level had a number of minutes of homework that could be assigned. This was disturbing on several levels. The teachers with the loudest voices got to assign more homework and those who were timid got to assign less. The teachers' needs were put first and good pedagogy was not a part of the conversation.

Hopefully, not all homework committee meetings are not as dysfunctional as those that I attended. The utter craziness of assigning homework based on time is that no teacher can tell how long it will take for each student to do their homework. If a math teacher assigns 10 problems, one student will complete them in 10 minutes, another in 20, and some possibly an hour. Homework policies based on time are an exercise in futility if teachers are teaching using traditional methods. Timed policies punish students who are slower learners, who often don't have the parental support at home, and who just fall farther and farther behind.

The benefit of a flipped class video is that the time is known. These short, teacher-created or curated videos have a known time quantity. Creating a homework policy based on time is feasible when a flipped video is assigned. If a flipped video is eight minutes long, plan on 12 to 14 minutes of homework. That's it! Flipped video homework is a simple way to know with a fair degree of precision how long students will spend on homework. And now those homework committee meetings, rather than being spent fighting for student home time, can be spent discussing the pedagogy of good homework—or possibly eliminated.

SETTING UP YOUR SCHOOL FOR FLIPPED HOMEWORK: TECHNOLOGY

I feel that a systemic approach to flipped learning is needed. While flipped learning can be executed by one teacher in a class with little support from administrators, that is not ideal. It is time for schools, and especially school leaders, to set up their technology infrastructure in such a way that it maximizes successful adoption of flipped learning.

I have consulted with many schools and one thing I have noticed is that schools that take an intentional approach to implementing the flipped classroom model run relatively smoothly. Because flipped learning has primarily been a grassroots movement, the first teachers to adopt the model often use a variety of technological tools to both create and organize video content.

There are a wide variety of video creation tools and software available, and many claim to be the best tool to flip a class. The fact is that *there really is no one best tool.* In my experience, the best flipped class rollouts happen when a school or district focuses their professional development efforts on just a few tools. When selecting the right tool, a school should select a tool that is "crazy easy" to use and interfaces with its technology infrastructure.

To organize videos, most teachers use one of many learning management systems—for example, Canvas, Schoology, Edmodo, Google Classroom, Haiku Learning, Blackboard, 1Know, and eChalk. However, as teachers increasingly adopt the flipped class model, each using a different learning management system, it creates confusion for students (who, for example, may have three flipped classes with three different learning management systems). Although each of these tools is helpful, having so many options may create confusion for staff as well. Professional development also suffers because technology trainers have to be able to work on any and all platforms. Thus, it is much easier to have one learning management system for your entire school—which will simplify things for students and staff, simplify professional development, and ensure wider adoption of flipped learning. (I recently created a course entitled "How to Avoid the 17 Deadly Sins of Flipped Learning Technology Selection," which can be accessed for free at http://learn.flglobal.org.)

SUPPORT FOR SCHOOL TO HELP UNDERSERVED POPULATIONS

The fundamental shift that the flipped classroom provides is that it helps students who often go home to a place where they do not have a support structure to help them with difficult homework—students from underserved populations. When such students are assigned traditional homework or higher-level activities, without the proper support structure at home, they try to solve a problem, get stuck, and simply give up. A short flipped video taught at the knowledge or understanding level can go a long way in helping underserved students.

The big question about students who come from underserved populations is, what about access? Doesn't the flipped classroom model hinge upon students having access to the Internet at home, and what if students don't have that access? Good leadership on the school or district level can help alleviate this issue. The good news is that by 2019, 99 percent of all schools in the United States will have high-speed Internet—thanks to the ConnectED Initiative spearheaded by President Barack Obama in 2014. As part of the initiative, free or significantly reduced-cost high-speed internet will be provided to students from low-income families.

For those students who do not have outside access to the Internet, a number of solutions can be employed:

- *Point students in the direction of available access.* You may be surprised at how many students, even those in economically disadvantaged areas, have ready access to the Internet. Many have portable devices (for example, smartphones), Wi-Fi-ready devices (for example, an iPod or tablet), or some other device. Students often simply need a place where they can connect to Wi-Fi. It is rare to find a business in the United States that does not provide free Wi-Fi.

- *Provide Wi-Fi and instruction.* As schools get more and more wired, students without Wi-Fi at home can access flipped video content at school and download it onto their personal devices or school-supplied devices. I have worked with a number of schools with student-access issues. Students with limited access to the Internet are instructed on how to download flipped video content onto a portable device.

- *Open up your school.* Most schools have computers in computer labs, libraries, and other common areas. If a school is going to embrace the flipped classroom model, those areas should be staffed before school, during lunch, and after school. Students will flock to those area to get an Internet connection. Some schools even provide Wi-Fi on school busses.

- *Explore the community.* Many businesses and most public libraries provide free Wi-Fi. Take the time to visit various establishments in the community and compile and distribute to students a list of those that offer free Wi-Fi. You could even find out from students the names and locations of the establishments that they frequent and have them serve as the points of contact with community partners.

- *Consider DVDs.* Students without access to an Internet-enabled device may likely have access to a TV with a DVD player. Videos can easily be burned onto DVDs and handed out to students—as Aaron Sams and I did when we pioneered the flipped class in our school in 2007 (as we found that every student at least had a DVD player at home).

I realize that the issue of access is an important one. If you have one student with limited access, you need to address the issue. I have worked with schools that have upwards of 80 percent free- and reduced-lunch populations that have figured out how to make this work. They had to be creative, but they made it work because they realize how beneficial it is for their students.

SUPPORTING INNOVATIVE TEACHERS

Taking a risk by stepping out and implementing flipped learning is new and different. The first teachers to embrace flipped learning in a school are brave. They break with tradition and try something new, and they deserve support and respect. Creating a place where risk and innovation are supported is something leadership should foster. This happens as administrators believe in teachers and empower them. This requires that administrators support innovative teachers and then figure out how to replicate the efforts of such teachers. Every administrator knows which teachers in their school are positive leaders. They should do whatever it takes to get those teachers what they need, have them as allies, and then have them help transform the school one teacher at a time.

MODELING FLIPPED LEARNING: FLIPPED MEETINGS

Not only do teachers have face-to-face time with their students, administrators also have such time with teachers—it's called a faculty meeting. Too often, faculty meetings are used for information dissemination instead of for engaging in rich discussions of best practices or a collaborative time of inquiry and learning. An administrator who really wants teachers to start incorporating the flipped classroom model should serve as a model of good pedagogical practice—and teachers who lead departments, PLC, and IEP meetings should do the same.

The objective of a flipped faculty meeting is to have deeper and more meaningful experiences during face-to-face meetings. I have seen two different approaches to flipped faculty meetings:

1. In one approach, teachers watch a short informational video (or simply read an e-mail or article) that contains information on things such as the upcoming basketball game, the policy changes, or the testing schedule. That done, the faculty meeting time is devoted to things such as teachers sharing best practices, small group conversations about things such as new standards, or a proposed new schedule.

2. Administrators have teaching roles too. They want teachers to learn new things, which will, in turn, help the students in their school become successful. In this approach, administrators create a video (which provides background and context for staff) or read an article about, for example, the implications of common core curricula for their staff. Then during the meeting, the teachers use the background provided in the video as the basis of an activity or discussion.

Approximately two years ago at a conference, I challenged administrators to flip their faculty meetings and Paul Hermes, associate principal at Bay View Middle School, in Wisconsin, took up the challenge. He flipped his staff meetings with great success. He reports that he was able to get 24 more hours of professional learning time with his faculty over the course of a year. Paul reports that flipped faculty meetings completely transformed his school climate. To learn more about Paul's experience with flipped faculty meetings, read his guest blog on my site at http://bit.ly/flipstaff.

COMMUNICATING WITH PARENTS

Most parents are not aware of the flipped classroom model and will need some information. They may hear from their students such things as, "My teacher is not teaching anymore" or "All we ever do is watch videos." It is imperative that administrators, along with key teacher leaders, communicate how the flipped classroom model will benefit students by providing extra time for teachers to interact with individual students. I have seen this happen in a number of ways:

- Teachers sending letters home (see such a letter in the Appendix).
- Schools communicating with parents via e-mail, letters, and so on.
- Schools holding informational meetings.
- Teachers/schools flipping the open house night (parents watch a short video on the flipped class and then discuss it during the open house, thus flipping the open house).

Ultimately this is a communication issue. As with any new initiative in a school, communication is of paramount importance.

HELPING PARENTS HELP THEIR KIDS

When I first started flipping my classes in 2007, I had parents come and tell me how much they loved my flipped videos. At first I was shocked that my parents were watching my flipped class videos. But as time went on and I began to train other teachers in this method, I realized this was not uncommon. Scores of parents were watching the video content alongside their children. This led me to realize that there are some really good ways for parents to help their children with homework in a flipped class.

I encourage parents to occasionally watch the videos with their children. This will help students not only complete the homework, but will model an interest in what they are learning at school. As parents interact with the video content in this way, they will learn the content being taught at the school and be able to help their child. Though students may know how to watch a video, they often don't know how to watch an educational video for understanding. Following are ways that parents can help their children get the most out of flipped class homework:

- *Organize notes or reflections.* Many students don't know how to organize their thoughts on paper. When a parent works with their child on note-taking, a student acquires a valuable skill that he will use later in life.
- *Ensure distraction-free viewing.* Since most of the videos are posted online, it is easy for students to get distracted by any number of other online activities. When parents ensure students are watching the video for their homework, students will be more successful.
- *Frame good questions.* Students often don't know what to ask when they interact with new content. Parents can help out by prompting their children to develop deeper questions that they can ask in school.

The Appendix contains a checklist for students about how best to watch flipped videos. It offers specific advice regarding the setting, how best to take notes, and how to effectively participate in a flipped classroom.

I wrote a blog post aimed at parents, entitled "Five Reasons Parents Should Be Thrilled their Child Is in a Flipped Class" (http://bit.ly/Parents Flip) in which I chronicle the benefits of both flipped homework and flipped learning:

- *Reason #1: It will increase student-teacher interaction.* There is something I fundamentally believe about good teaching: it is about developing good relationships between the teacher and the student. One of the beauties of the flipped classroom is that it gives the teacher more individual time with each student. That means your son or daughter will get more one-on-one time with his teacher. There is something powerful about moving the teacher away from the "front of the room." Getting teachers in and among their students changes the dynamics of the class. When we flipped our classes in 2007, I knew my students better than I had in my previous 19 years as a teacher. Spending lots of quality time with each child helped me to know my students better, both cognitively and relationally.

- *Reason #2: It will help you help your child.* How many times has your child come home with homework they were unable to understand? You sat with them at the dinner table and tried as much as possible to help them, but you couldn't. Or maybe you had learned something when you were in school, and your child has informed you that you "do it wrong." One of the beauties of the flipped classroom is that you, too, can watch the videos with your kids. You can learn how the teacher teaches a topic and you will be better equipped to help your son or daughter.

- *Reason #3: It will decrease the anxiety of your child over home-work.* I have three children and there have been times when our kids came home with homework and they were stressed. They had too much to do and either not enough time or not enough understanding. That, in some cases, led our children to tears and my wife and I to much wringing of our hands. If the homework is for the students to watch and interact with a short video (I strongly emphasize that the video needs to be SHORT!), then this is much more doable. The idea is for the kids to do the hard stuff in class.

- *Reason #:4 Your child will be able to pause and rewind their teacher.* In one of the early years of the flipped classroom, my daughter Kaitie was watching a video of me in my living room (which, by the way, is weird), and she jumped up and said, "I love the flipped classroom." I asked her why and she said, "Because I get to pause you." I was taken aback, but I realized what she was saying. She could pause her teacher. All kids learn at different speeds and, frankly, we teachers talk too fast. Wouldn't it be great if your son or daughter could pause and rewind their teacher? Well, if they are in a flipped classroom, they can do just that.

- *Reason #5: It will lead your child to deeper learning.* There is one thing I have seen happen with almost every teacher who has flipped their classroom: they flip their classroom for about one to two years and then they go beyond the flipped classroom to deeper-learning strategies—for example, project-based learning, challenge-based learning, and mastery learning. Count yourself extremely fortunate if you have a teacher who has flipped their class for multiple years. These teachers have no doubt completely changed the dynamic of their classrooms. Their students, instead of being focused on test preparation or busywork, are actively engaged in their own learning, taking responsibility for their learning, and enthusiastically embracing learning.

Parents are no longer expected to be the expert at home. The role of the parent has changed. Parents need to encourage their children to interact deeply with the flipped class videos. It really is that simple. I have heard from countless parents from schools around the world who have thanked me profusely for taking the fight, or shall we say, for transforming homework so that it is no longer the "H" word.

06

CHAPTER 6
TYING IT ALL TOGETHER

I recently received an e-mail from my friend Troy Stein, who was frustrated with his daughter's science class. His daughter had fallen behind, and he was trying to get her caught up. He acknowledged that his daughter had made some poor choices that resulted in her being behind, but at the time of the e-mail, she was ready to learn. The class was on chapter four, while Troy's daughter still did not understand key concepts from chapter one. Troy was on a mission. He realized that it had been a long time since he'd taken 9th grade physical science, but since he was a smart man with a Master's degree working in the IT field, he figured he could learn enough to help his daughter.

Troy took the textbook, made notecards, and did some problems in an attempt to learn the material. But in the end, Troy was unable to help his daughter. He realized that the information was not going to come easily for him. He then hired a tutor, which didn't help. In frustration, he posted a YouTube video addressed to the school's science department. Refreshingly, in the video, he blames neither the teachers nor the content. Rather, he questions the design of a traditional classroom. He ponders why, in the case of traditional classroom homework, the hard stuff is being done in the worst place—at home—when the students are home away from the real expert—the teacher. Troy then wonders what it would be like if his daughter had grown up in a place where parental support was low, or even nonexistent. What chance would somebody like his daughter have? He concludes the video by sharing with the science faculty how he has seen the flipped class and, more importantly, how flipped mastery transform classrooms and schools. (If you would like to see Troy's thoughtful video, go to http://bit.ly/parentfliphw.)

The value of homework is a hot topic in the education world right now. When homework is done well, it increases student achievement. One way to take some of the stigma out of the "H" word is to adopt the flipped classroom model and follow the advice in this book. Instead of sending students home to do the "hard stuff," we need to send the lower-level cognitive tasks home so that when students come to class, they can work on the higher-order cognitive tasks with an expert—their teacher. In this way, students will have a richer and more meaningful in-class experience. Another way to say this is: homework is the place for the light lifting and class time is the place for the heavy lifting. As educators, we need to stop sending the hard stuff home, where students may not have the ability or the support to complete the assignment. Instead, we need to have techniques that will help all students be successful and engaged learners. Flipped learning simplifies the entire homework experience. Students' homework is purposeful, efficient, efficacious, and aesthetically appealing.

We have to rethink homework! We must make it more meaningful and effective! We have to stop using homework to beat up students for noncompliance or for simply reinforcing the status quo. What we need is to transform how we assign homework. Through flipped videos, homework becomes a pathway to deeper engagement, understanding, and learning.

Some teachers say they have tried the flipped class by attempting a few lessons and then, when many students do not watch the flipped video, they decide it just doesn't work for their kids. These teachers say, "They won't do it!" Then they revert to the lecture style because they feel their students will at least get something out of the traditional model. As educators, we understand that nothing comes easy the first time. And trying the flipped class is no different. Don't just give it a try for a few lessons and throw it out. Stick with it and believe that it will work. Don't approach it with the attitude that you will just try and if your students don't like it you'll go back to your old method. Walk into your room with confidence and say, "Students, we need to go deeper and learn better, and the method we will be using will be the flipped class model." Start with confidence and poise.

Change is hard! Stick with it! And I promise that you will not look back.

APPENDIX

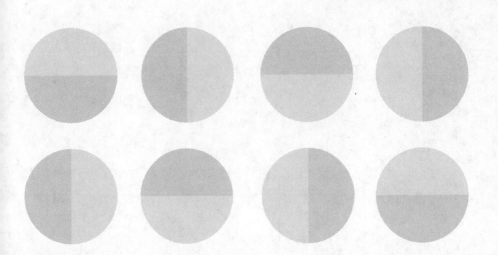

HOW TO WATCH A FLIPPED VIDEO: GUIDELINES FOR STUDENTS

The following guidelines, which teachers may hand out to students, are designed to help students prepare for a flipped video assignment:

The flipped classroom requires you to take more responsibility for your learning. Make sure to follow these guidelines when doing flipped homework.

Setting

- I am sitting in a place that is quiet and free of distractions.
- I have silenced my phone.
- I have closed all other tabs and windows on my device.
- I am not connected to social media while watching the flipped video.
- I have my class notebook and a writing device to take notes.
- I use headphones when I watch the video (to increase my focus).

Notetaking

- I take careful notes as I watch the video.
- I draw appropriate diagrams and charts in my notes.
- I frequently pause the video to take notes.
- I rewind the video when I don't understand things.
- I pause the video and solve a problem or write something down when my teacher tells me to do so.
- I answer the questions asked in the video to the best of my ability.
- I write down questions in my notes from the flipped video when I don't understand something.
- I take my questions to class.

In Class

- I ask my teacher the questions I wrote down in my notes so that I can receive help and clarification.

- I fully participate in class activities.
- I collaborate with my peers.
- I offer to help my peers with things I understand.
- I get help from my peers when they understand more than I do.

VIDEO EXEMPLARS

Though it is best practices to have teachers create their own flipped videos, it is useful to look at a variety of other videos as a guide. Following are notes on and links to quality flipped videos:

SUBJECT/ LEVEL	NOTES	LINK
All/All	As Jon has been curating, and has received, teachers' flipped class channels for several years, the flipped class video repository contains more than 100 video channels.	bit.ly/flipvid1
All/3rd grade	The website of Randy Brown, who has more than 500 videos that he uses for flipping his 3rd grade class.	MrRBrown.org
Science/High School	Paul Andersen has created hundreds of high-quality science videos.	bozemanscience.com
Physics/High School	Jonathan Thomas-Palmer has created very high quality flipped videos. Note: Don't be intimidated by the videos (as most flipped videos have much lower production value).	flippingphysics.com
Math/5th grade	Delia Bush is an award-winning elementary teacher.	bit.ly/flipvid2
Math/High School	John Tague's YouTube channel	bit.ly/flipvid3
Math/High School	Michael Moore's YouTube channel	bit.ly/flipvid4
Language Arts/ Middle School and High School	Andrew Thomasson and Cheryl Morris' YouTube Channel	bit.ly/flipvid5

SUBJECT/ LEVEL	NOTES	LINK
Literacy/K–2	Carol Redmond's website	carolredmond. blogspot.com
History/High School	Tom Driscoll's YouTube channel	bit.ly/flipvid6
World Languages/All grades	Señora Dill's website for teaching Spanish and French to English-speaking students.	senora-dill.wikispaces. com
High School and AP Psychology	Don Meyers' You Tube channel	bit.ly/flipvid7
Biology/High School	Jeremy LeCornu, a teacher in Australia, has some amazing videos with some innovative techniques.	bit.ly/flipvid8
Math and Business/High School	Joel Speranza uses a "forward board" to make his videos, which are very engaging.	bit.ly/flipvid9

FEEDBACK ON THE FLIPPED CLASS: STUDENT SURVEY

Student feedback can inform teachers about how to improve a flipped classroom. Following are some sample questions that can act as a catalyst as you work to create your own survey. You may also want your students to add to the survey referred to in this book (which may be found at http://bit.ly/fliphw).

1. At what time of the day do you watch the flipped videos?
   a. Right before class
   b. In the morning
   c. During school time
   d. Right after school
   e. In the evening

2. Do you multitask while watching the flipped videos?
   a. I never multitask during flipped videos
   b. I sometimes multitask during flipped videos
   c. I often multitask during flipped videos
   d. I always multitask during flipped videos

3. How does the flipped homework system compare to traditional teacher systems?
   a. Worse: Worksheets/textbook pages would be much better than watching videos.
   b. OK, but: It's better in a few ways, but worse in some other ways.
   c. No opinion: It's basically the same.
   d. Better: Overall, it is a good idea.
   e. Great: I totally prefer this system. More teachers should do this!

4. How easily could you access and watch videos before the due date? (It would be best if the responses to this question were based on a scale of 1 to 5, with 1 being "Never a problem at all.")

   a. Very tough. I often had difficulty getting to watch the videos at home or at school on time.

   b. Never a problem at all! I always had enough time and easy access to the Internet.

5. How should I improve the videos (choose all that apply)?

   a. Fewer words on screen

   b. Talk/act less dramatically on screen

   c. More words on screen

   d. Have all videos follow the same format

   e. More "voiceover" videos where we can't see your face

   f. Make them more interactive by asking us questions

   g. Change nothing! They're fine!

   h. Talk/act more dramatically on screen

   i. More "live" videos where we can see you talk to the camera

   j. Other:

6. How happy are you with the presentation of the videos (e.g., voiceover, color choice, content)?

   a. Not happy

   b. Somewhat happy

   c. Happy

   d. Very happy

7. How did you usually watch the homework videos?

   a. On a cell phone

   b. On a computer at home

   c. On a computer at school

   d. Other:

8. Over the entire school year, did you watch videos before the due date (please be honest)?

    a. Rarely

    b. About half the time

    c. Not at first, but more later in the year

    d. Most of the time

    e. Always

9. How often did you watch the videos that were suggested in class?

    a. Almost always

    b. More than half the times suggested

    c. Less than half the times suggested

    d. Never

10. Where did you usually watch the flipped videos?

    a. At home

    b. In our class

    c. During school (another class, lunch, etc.)

11. Has using the videos allowed your teacher to spend more time with you or in smaller groups in the classroom?

    a. All of the time

    b. Most of the time

    c. Some of the time

    d. Rarely

12. Do you watch flipped videos one at a time or in batches?

13. What is one thing that you like about the flipped videos?

14. What do you like about class activities?

15. What would you change about class activities?

16. What advice about this class would you give to next year's students (in other words, what do you wish someone had told you last September)?

17. What would the class be missing if we went to a traditional/lecture-based classroom?

18. How have the online videos supported your learning of this topic?

A special thanks goes to the following teachers who contributed survey questions: Andrew Swan, Jill McClean, Robert Glenn, and Kelly Hollis.

INTRODUCING FLIPPED LEARNING: LETTER TO PARENTS

As parents will likely want to know about flipped learning, and why their children are watching videos instead of doing their homework, it might be helpful to send a letter such as the following to the parents of your students before the beginning of the school year.

Parents:

I am excited that your son or daughter is in my class this year. This is my 24th year teaching and I still love my job. Working with your children keeps me young and teaching has been the calling of my life.

This letter is not your typical introductory letter, where I give the syllabus and the grading policy—which you can find at http://myschool.com/mrteacher, if you're interested. Instead, I would like to share with you what I believe about education, and then explain how that philosophy flows to the methods I will be using to teach your children.

As I have read educational research, I feel it can be summarized into two big take-aways:

1. Students learn best when they have positive interactions and relationships with their teachers and with their peers.

2. Students learn best when learning is active and engaging.

To that end, I have adopted the "flipped classroom" approach to learning—the best way to ensure deeper relationships and a more active classroom.

In a nutshell, the model involves students doing their homework via interacting with short micro-videos—which replace the direct teaching (lecture) portion of the class. And when your son or daughter comes to class, they will apply and expand upon what was introduced in the micro-video. The reason the model is called the flipped classroom is that what used to be done at home (typical homework) is done in class and what was typically done in class (lecture) is done at home.

The flipped classroom model is being adopted by teachers across the globe with very good results. I have found it especially helpful in my classes because it has freed me up to spend more individual time with my students (your sons and daughters), helped students take more ownership of their learning, and increased student performance on exams.

Gone are the days when your son or daughter comes home with a homework assignment that they can't do. Their primary homework is to interact and take notes on these short micro-videos I have made. The videos are between four and 12 minutes long and should take your son or daughter no more than 20 minutes.

If you have questions about the model, I encourage you to watch this short video (which you can find at http://bit.ly/explainflip) made by one of the experts in flipped learning—Jon Bergmann. This video explains the model well and will give you a good idea of what my class will be like. Also, feel free to reach out to me at school via e-mail or phone.

I look forward to teaching your sons and daughters this school year.

Mr. Teacher
jteacher@myschool.com
303-333-3333, X3333

FLIPPED VIDEO CREATION: CHECKLIST

The vast majority of teachers who flip their classes leverage video for the prework. The following checklist will help you as you prepare to create your flipped video.

Technology

- The video is recorded in a quiet room.
- The video has annotations (drawings).
- The video is posted online.
- Students know how to access the video content.

Video Content

- The video is short.
- The video contains one topic.
- The video is set up for interaction.
- The video has questions embedded and requires students to respond to several prompts.
- The video introduces new content.
- The video is at the knowledge or understanding level in Bloom's Taxonomy.
- The video has more pictures than words.

Other Considerations

- The video is created with a colleague (when possible).
- I speak with energy.
- I speak in a conversational tone.
- I have included my face in the video.
- The video has been planned to meet curricular objectives.
- All images from other sources are cited.

ADVANCED ORGANIZER: EXAMPLE

Advanced organizers, sometimes called follow-along sheets, are used by many teachers in conjunction with the flipped video assignments. The following is an example of a follow-along sheet for an AP chemistry class (noting that the actual follow-along sheet included more space for students to insert notes).

VIDEO 6.1: THERMOCHEMISTRY

First Law of Thermodynamics

Energy cannot _____

The sum total of energy in the universe _____

Thermodynamics means (examine the word)

Energy in a Chemical Reaction

Energy can flow two ways in a reaction

Into: Endothermic

Out: Exothermic

Called Enthalpy: Symbol is ΔH

Four Ways to Calculate ΔH (Fill in the Chart below)

Four Ways to Calculate ΔH

_____   _____

PROGRESS MONITORING SHEET

Shane Ferguson, a middle school teacher in Ohio, has students self-monitor their progress by completing the following form, a great tool for student self-reflection and self-advocacy as they progress through a section.

HONORS MATH 7

NAME:

TOPIC/UNIT: **Topic 3/4: Rational and Irrational Numbers**

COMMON CORE STANDARDS:

8.NS.1: Know that numbers that are not rational are called irrational. Understand informally that every number has a decimal expansion; for rational numbers show that the decimal expansion repeats eventually, and convert a decimal expansion which repeats eventually into a rational number.

8.NS.2: Use rational approximations of irrational numbers to compare the size of irrational numbers, locate them approximately on a number line diagram, and estimate the value of expressions (e.g., $\pi 2$). For example, by truncating the decimal expansion of $\sqrt{2}$, show that $\sqrt{2}$ is between 1 and 2, then between 1.4 and 1.5, and explain how to continue on to get better approximations.

PRE-TEST SCORE: _____

Reflection (What did you do well on? What did you struggle with most?):

My goal for my post-test is:

My plan to achieve my post-test goal is to:

Midpoint Reflection

How am I doing at the halfway point? What can I do to continue toward my goal or what do I need to complete on time?

Assignments Due:

ORDER	ASSIGNMENT	I CAN / REFLECTION
	Online Games (Fractions, Decimals, Percents)	
	Square Root Tarsia Cards	
	Topic 3/4 Mixed Review	
	Topic 3/4 Assignment	
	Topic 3/4 Assessment Practice	
	Summer Olympic Activity Application	
	Skyscraper Activity Application	

POST-TEST SCORE: _____

Reflection (Did I meet my goal? What did I learn? What can I do to improve or maintain on the next unit?):

BIBLIOGRAPHY

Anderson, L.W., & Krathwohl, D. R. (2001). *A taxonomy for learning, teaching, and assessing: A revision of bloom's taxonomy of educational objectives*. New York: Longman.

Bergmann, J., & Sams, A. (2012). *Flip your classroom: Reach every student in every class every day*. Eugene, Or.: International Society for Technology in Education.

Bergmann, J., & Sams, A. (2014). *Flipped learning: Gateway to student engagement*. Eugene Oregon: International Society for Technology in Education.

Cooper, H. M. (2001). *Battle over homework: Common ground for administrators, teachers, and parents* (2nd ed.). Thousand Oaks, CA: Corwin Press.

Epstein, J. L., Davis, S.M., Logan, E., Moore, T.E., Myers, T.N., Cole, C., Hammonds, J., & Taylor, J. (1992). *TIPS: teachers involve parents in schoolwork: Interactive homework in language arts: Prototype activities, grade 7*. Baltimore, MD: Center on Families, Communities, Schools, and Children's Learning, Johns Hopkins U.

Epstein, J.L., Salinas, K.C., & Jackson, V.E. (1995). TIPS: Teachers involve parents in schoolwork: language arts, science/health, and math interactive homework in the middle grades. Baltimore, MD: Center on Families, Communities, Schools, and Children's Learning, Johns Hopkins U.

Galloway, M., Connor, J., & Pope, D. (2013). Nonacademic effects of homework in privileged, high-performing high schools. *The Journal of Experimental Education, 81*(4), 490–510.

Holland, B. (2014, November. The 4Ss of note-taking with technology. *Edutopia.* Retrieved from http://www.edutopia.org/blog/the-4ss-of-note-taking-beth-holland

iNACOL. (n.d.) What is competency education? Retrieved from http://www.competencyworks.org/wp-content/uploads/2014/11/CWorks-Understanding-Competency-Education.pdf.

Kohn, A. (2006). *The homework myth: Why our kids get too much of a bad thing.* Boston, MA: Da Capo Lifelong Books.

Kohn, A. (2009). Alfie Kohn: Making students work a 'second shift.' *YouTube.* Available at https://www.youtube.com/watch?v=npZ4dkt4e4U

Marzano, R. J. (2007). *The art and science of teaching: A comprehensive framework for effective instruction.* Alexandria, VA: ASCD.

Marzano, R. J., & Pickering, D. J. (2007). The case for and against homework. *Educational Leadership, 64*(6), 74–79.

Mazur, E. (1997). *Peer instruction: A user's manual.* Upper Saddle River, NJ: Prentice Hall.

McKibben, S. (2014). Mastering the flipped faculty meeting. *Education Update, 56*(1), 2–4.

Mueller, P. A., & Oppenheimer, D. M. (2014). The pen is mightier than the keyboard: Advantages of longhand over laptop notetaking. *Psychological Science 25*(6), 159–168.

Reeves, D. B. (2004). The case against the zero. *Phi Delta Kappan 86*(4), 324–25.

Reid, K.S. (2013). Survey finds half of parents struggle with their children's homework. *Education Week, 33*(4). Retrieved from http://blogs.edweek.org/edweek/parentsandthepublic/2013/09/half_of_parents_struggle_to_help_their_kids_with_homework_survey_finds.html

The White House. (2014). ConnectED: President obama's plan for connecting all schools to the digital age. Retrieved from https://www.whitehouse.gov/sites/default/files/docs/connected_fact_sheet.pdf.

Vatterott, C. (2009). *Rethinking homework: Best practices that support diverse needs.* Alexandria, VA: ASCD.

Vatterott, C. (2010). Five hallmarks of good homework. *Educational Leadership, 68*(1), 10–15.

Weir, K. (2016). Is homework a necessary evil? *Monitor on Psychology, 47*(3), 36.

Wikipedia. (n.d.). Peer Instruction. Wikimedia Foundation. Retrieved from https://en.wikipedia.org/wiki/Peer_instruction

INDEX

ABOUT THE AUTHOR

 **Jonathan Bergmann** is one of the pioneers of the Flipped Classroom Movement. He is leading the worldwide adoption of flipped learning through the Flipped Learning Global Initiative (FLGI) (flglobal. org). He works with government entities, schools, corporations, and education nonprofits. Jon has coordinated and guided flipped learning projects in the United States and around the globe—China, Taiwan, Korea, Australia, the Middle East, Iceland, Sweden, Norway, the United Kingdom, Italy, Spain, Mexico, Canada, and South America.

Jonathan spent 24 years as a middle and high school science teacher before becoming the lead technology facilitator for a school district in the Chicago suburbs, is the author of seven books, including the bestselling book *Flip Your Classroom*, which has been translated into 13 languages, and is the founder of the global FlipCon conferences, dynamic engaging events that inspire educators to transform their instructional practices through flipped learning.

In 2002, Jonathan received the Presidential Award for Excellence for Math and Science Teaching, in 2010 was named semi-finalist for Colorado Teacher of the Year, and in 2013 was named one of Tech & Learning's 10 Most Influential People of the Year, was a finalist for the Brock International Prize for Education, and won the Bammy Award, presented by the Academy of Education Arts and Sciences.

Jonathan serves on the advisory board for TED-Education, hosts the radio show *The Flip Side,* has a popular YouTube channel with more than three million views, and has a very active blog where he discusses flipped learning best practices. You can learn more at JonBergmann.com.

RELATED RESOURCES

At the time of publication, the following ASCD resources were available (ASCD stock numbers appear in parentheses). For up-to-date information about ASCD resources, go to www.ascd.org. You can search the complete archives of Educational Leadership at http://www.ascd.org/el.

ASCD Edge Group

Exchange ideas and connect with other educators interested in inclusion on the social networking site ASCDEdge® at http://ascdedge.ascd.org/.

Print Products

Flip Your Classroom: Reach Every Student in Every Class Every Day by Jonathan Bergmann and Aaron Sams (#112060)

Education Update: Tips to Help You Flip Your Classroom (February 2013) (#113047)

Educational Leadership: Technology-Rich Learning (March 2013) (#113037)

Educational Leadership: Instruction That Sticks (October 2014) (#115017)

Education Update: Syllabus-ted: Preparing Students for the Rigors of College Reading (July 2016) (#116052)

Educational Leadership: The Working Lives of Educators (May 2016) (#116035)

Educational Leadership: Looking at Student Work (April 2016) (#116034)

Educational Leadership: Helping ELLs Excel (February 2016) (#116032)

Educational Leadership: Professional Learning: Reimagined (May 2014) (#114025)

Educational Leadership: Getting Students to Mastery (December 2013) (#114021)

For more information, send e-mail to member@ascd.org; call 1-800-933-2723 or 703-578-9600; send a fax to 703-575-5400; or write to Information Services, ASCD, 1703 N. Beauregard St., Alexandria, VA 22311-1714 USA.